PEORIA'S
HAUNTED MEMORIES

PEORIA'S
HAUNTED MEMORIES

Stephanie E. McCarthy

ARCADIA
PUBLISHING

Copyright © 2009 by Stephanie E. McCarthy
ISBN 978-0-7385-6008-3

Published by Arcadia Publishing
Charleston, South Carolina

Printed in the United States of America

Library of Congress Control Number: 2009927171

For all general information contact Arcadia Publishing at:
Telephone 843-853-2070
Fax 843-853-0044
E-mail sales@arcadiapublishing.com
For customer service and orders:
Toll-Free 1-888-313-2665

Visit us on the Internet at www.arcadiapublishing.com

Contents

PREFACE

Peoria's Haunted Memories presents supernatural tales and popular folklore of the city of Peoria and the surrounding area. These are stories of horrifying apparitions, grisly murders, cursed ground, haunted houses, ghostly retribution, and unnatural coincidences. Peoria is a town of rumor and truth—a place of shadow and mirrors where local history has been colorized by unsavory gangsters, dark deeds, murder, corruption, and political controversy. It is also a place of undeniable beauty and dignity, where education and religion have been honored and revered. Ghost stories, folktales, and legends have their own unique historical significance. This book is not solely intended to educate the reader on the history of Peoria but rather to provide a different perspective of that history through some of the supernatural stories and folklore that bind our community. The historical locations are home to many different entities and provide a glimpse of Peoria's colorful past that will appeal to readers of all ages. The places presented in this compilation are real. If you travel to these sites, please observe any local rules or laws regarding trespassing and have respect for the history of the area.

ACKNOWLEDGMENTS

In creating this book, the author has talked to many individuals and visited local sites related to purported supernatural activity. The author would like to acknowledge and thank the Peoria Historical Society and its members for all their work in the maintenance and preservation of the history of the Peoria area. The author would also like to thank the employees of the Peoria Public Library for their assistance. On a personal note, the author gives special thanks to her husband, Tim McCarthy; mother, Elizabeth Zentz; grandfather John Armstrong; and all the family and friends who have been tireless supporters of this endeavor. Without their assistance this book would not have been possible. Unless otherwise noted, all images are from the author's collection.

Adams Street is seen here, looking north from Main Street in 1888. (Courtesy of the Peoria Public Library, Oakford Collection.)

INTRODUCTION

I don't believe in ghosts but I'm afraid of them.

—Mark Twain

People love a good scare. In a recent poll, it was determined that 48 percent of the American public believes in ghosts. If that percentage is surprising, perhaps even more so is that 22 percent of Americans claim to have personally seen or felt the presence of a supernatural presence. Recounting such experiences has historically been a popular way to bind humanity in its mortal struggle and establish a kinship with those still living. The ghost story has its roots in legend and folklore and is traditionally passed down as part of local history. Many of these stories have expanded beyond their localities to become part of the national consciousness.

The ghost story flourished between 1880 and 1930, when the fashion for spiritualism was at its height. The promise of communion with the dead held great appeal at a time of religious uncertainty and Darwinian theories of evolution. Popular writers of the time took advantage of this fascination and aided the public in its pursuit of supernatural interests by creating ghostly specters, creaking houses, and cemeteries cloaked in shrouds of darkness.

Ghost stories are cathartic. They require a childlike faith in the intangible and provide the grown-up realization that nothing is really going to happen, that the dark and fantastic shadows will resume their familiar shapes in the daylight. People remain enraptured and fascinated by the unknown, by the uncharted frontiers of the imagination that can reduce even the most wizened psyche to childlike wonderment.

Peoria is the largest city on the Illinois River and one of the oldest settlements in the state. It is a river city, with majestic bluffs spread along its sprawling banks. The history of the Peoria area dates back to 10,000 BC, when a large Native American civilization inhabited the area. The Illini Indian Confederacy settled in the area in the mid-1600s, with the Peoria, Kaskaskia, Cahokia, Tamaroa, and Michigamea people living here in harmony. Peoria's picturesque beauty was first noted by Fr. Jacques Marquette, a French Jesuit missionary, and Louis Joliet, a Quebecois, following its European discovery in 1673. The area's commanding vistas still entice visitors just as they must have done during the time of the first explorers. Marquette referred to the area as the Illinois valley for fertility and remarked that it was unparalleled in the abundance of natural wildlife.

In 1679, a second expedition led by Robert Cavalier de LaSalle visited the area with Henri Tonti, his second in command, and a group of 33 men. Also accompanying the group was Louis Hennepin, one of three Franciscan priests. They reached Lake Pimiteoni (Peoria Lake) and the camps of the Illini tribe. Robert Cavalier de LaSalle built Fort Creve Couer on the opposite side of the river approximately three miles south of the original landing site. After the group left, Fort Creve Couer was attacked and destroyed. The exact location of Fort Creve Couer remains a mystery and is the subject of intense debate among local historians.

In 1721, Fr. Pierre Francois Xavier de Charlevoix reported a visit to the village of Peoria and encountered at least four Frenchmen living with the Native Americans. He described the location as the same as that of the old village of Peoria that was established between 1673 and 1723 on the west bank of the Illinois River, south of Peoria Lake. In 1750, there is reference to a French fort and mission at Peoria. In 1756, a stockade was built in the area of this fort to help defend traders against Native American attacks. At that time, there were approximately 700 traders in the area. In 1763, the Illinois territory was ceded by the French to England.

From 1763 to 1778, the old village of Peoria was referred to as Old Peoria's Fort and Village and existed between what is now Caroline and Hayward Streets, bounded by Monroe Street to the west and the Illinois River to the east. During the 1760s, Jean Baptiste Maillet, a French Canadian, assumed a leadership role in the village. This first European settlement in Illinois consisted of French hunters and farmers as well as Native American traders. In 1773, Maillet sold his property to Jean Baptiste Pointe du Sable, Peoria's most notable black pioneer, who later became one of the first settlers in the new town of Chicago.

The old village of Peoria in the late 1700s consisted of a French military post, trading establishment, and an associated Native American village. French artifacts from the village were recovered from Detweiler Marina in 1882; however, the specific location of the French post and French settlement remains a mystery. In 1773, the old fort in Peoria was burned by local Fox Indian tribes.

Near the end of the 18th century, the site of the village of Peoria shifted from what is now the north bluff to the site of present-day downtown, about a mile and a half south of the old village on the edge of Peoria Lake. The reason attributed to the geographic shift was that the residents believed the water in Peoria Lake was fresher and thus healthier.

The early settlers often enlisted the help of the local Native Americans in construction of their buildings. At that time, the village boasted trading posts, a blacksmith shop, a chapel, a winepress, and a windmill. By 1818, there were many goods available for sale in central Illinois, including teakettles, combs, silk handkerchiefs, Indian muslin, stationery, handsaws, windowpanes, Dutch ovens, pans, and cutlery. There was also a large winery with huge wine vaults built underground. There are accounts that these wine vaults still exist under present-day downtown Peoria and in the 1920s were used by local gangsters during Prohibition.

Despite the inconveniences and hardships, the early settlers persevered, and slowly the population of the area grew. By 1825, there were over 20 log houses and 7 frame houses. As the area expanded, the town was laid out on a plat with the establishment of streets. Peoria eventually changed from a village to a rough frontier town, with 70–80 houses and 400–500 inhabitants.

The area continued to grow steadily, and on January 13, 1825, Peoria County was officially organized. From its earliest days, Peoria was a lawless town. Charles Ballance recorded the following remembrance of a real estate dispute and frontier justice, as reported by Jerry Klein in his book *Peoria*:

> Underhill (Isaac) some time ago threatened to tear down my garden fence, but from assurance I gave him he became apprehensive there might be some danger in (*sic*) and hired George Depree, a low-life bully, to do it. Depree undertook it three or four weeks ago when I was planting some things in the garden and I struck him a lick with the hoe which proved sufficient to stop him. On Monday late, Underhill hired an Irishman to do it and armed him with a pistol he himself guarding the man with a gun. As soon as I learned what was going

on, I went on the ground with a gun and two pistols. On my arrival, he cocked his gun and his man cocked his pistol. I ordered the man to desist from tearing down the fence. Underhill ordered him to proceed and raised his gun. At that instant I fired my gun at Underhill and he fired his at me and his man Thompson drew his pistol; but before he had time to shoot, I had fired a pistol at his head which made him retreat a short distance; but supposing I had no other pistol, he rallied with his pistol presented but seeing I was ready with another, he retreated. I then commenced reloading my gun upon which he approached me again with a cocked pistol but I kept him at bay with mine until I had loaded my gun. He then retreated and left the field, Underhill having retreated before. They then made complaint upon oath to a justice of the peace who after hearing their statements, ordered me to enter into bonds which I did for my appearance at the next circuit court since which time my fence has remained unmolested. During this day I was not only lame with the rheumatism, but also had a large blister of cathardies on my ankle insomuch that I had to fight on crutches but what made the case I was otherwise quite unwell.

After its incorporation on March 11, 1835, the town would be referred to as the Village of Peoria and was governed by a board of trustees. The population at the time of incorporation was 3,199. By 1840, that number had jumped to 7,041, and on May 5, 1845, Peoria was incorporated as a city. By 1857, the population had reached 7,482.

The Civil War began in 1861. A military training camp, Camp Lyon, was established on the east bluff for young men anxious to join the Illinois Volunteers. A second military training camp was later established on lower Spring Street. On June 10, 1861, the 17th Regiment of Volunteers took steamboats to Ottawa, en route to the Civil War battlefields. Five hundred and two Union soldiers from Peoria and Peoria County died in the Civil War, many of whom were later interred at Soldier's Hill in Springdale Cemetery.

In 1870, Charles Balance, a local attorney and historian, published his *History of Peoria*. At that time, there were over 20 specialty stores in the town, 12 drugstores, and 53 grocery stores. By 1872, the population of Peoria was 22,850.

The early products of Peoria were corn and corn-related products, so it was not surprising that whiskey distilleries soon sprang up throughout the city, eventually leading to Peoria's designation as the Whiskey Capital of the World. The production of whiskey brought unprecedented wealth to the area, and the whiskey barons constructed elaborate mansions along Moss Avenue and High Street, an area known as "High Wine." By 1887, there were 12 distilleries in Peoria, and this became the city's leading industry by the late 1800s, when the population had risen to over 50,000. The wealth generated by these distilleries was immense and allowed a small percentage of the population to live like royalty.

The whiskey business in Peoria proved highly profitable but also led to many civic problems. Easy women, cheap liquor, and games of chance fed the reputation of the "Saturday Night City." "I Wish I was in Peoria" was a popular tune among sailors as they reminisced on some of the high times they had in the river city. During its wild heyday, the downtown Peoria area abounded in gambling joints and bars: the Palace Club, the 101 Club, Mecca Supper Club, Pair-a-Dice Lounge, the Sportsman's Club, the Spot Tavern, the Stork Club, the Windsor Coffee Shop, and the Open Door welcomed the gamblers, criminals, and racketeers that called Peoria home. A famous nightclub called the Alps was built into a natural cave off Abingdon Street. Gamblers lined up three deep around the local crap and roulette tables.

In an interesting nod to propriety, women were not allowed in gambling establishments. However, they served other functions in the underworld, and there were at least three districts for prostitution on North Washington, South Jefferson, and Walnut Streets, and another near South Adams Street. Lillian Diamond, known as "Diamond Lil," ran a popular brothel at

200 Eaton Street. Although the whiskey era ended some of the greatest wealth the city had known, Peoria was well on its way to becoming a bustling metropolis. By 1940, the population of the city had reached 105,087.

Today the Peoria area is home to 370,000 residents. In addition to its booming industry and commerce, its beautiful recreational areas, and its unique shopping venues, Peoria also remains home to many ghosts, phantoms, and specters. In the early days of Peoria, superstitions and folklore abounded. Tales were told to explain the supernatural and to provide comfort to the living. Some of these stories continue to this day. Please enjoy this ghostly view of Peoria and the surrounding area.

One

NOW PLAYING IN PEORIA

I hold the world but as the world, Gratiano;
A stage where every man must play a part, and mine is a sad one.
—William Shakespeare, *The Merchant of Venice*, act 1, scene 1

The phrase "Will it play in Peoria?" became popular during the vaudeville era of the early 19th century. Peoria was seen as a barometer of public sentiment, and it was universally acknowledged by those in the theater world that if a production or show opened to strong reviews in Peoria, success was almost certainly guaranteed. If it did not "play" in Peoria, the production was either rewritten or cancelled. Over time, the phrase was adopted by promoters and politicians and became known throughout the nation. It became particularly well known during Pres. Richard Nixon's tenure in office, when the phrase was used as a gauge of the nation's feelings on social or economic issues. The meaning quickly spread to other areas, as Peoria became a popular testing ground for new products or advertisements. Even today, the city is viewed as representative of typical midwestern values, or Main Street America, and manufacturers continue to use Peoria to try out new products and advertisements.

Thanks to its early vaudeville history, Peoria already had a number of grand theaters by the time the talkies became popular in the early 20th century. The magnificent architecture and intricate art details of the local movie palaces were designed to awe the audience and make movie attendance a holiday. Excess was expected, and the movie palaces incorporated ornate arches and domed ceilings in styles ranging from oriental and art deco to Renaissance and Egyptian. This abundance of ornamentation was not merely for aesthetics. These theaters created a fantasy environment that effectively blocked out the realities of life and provided those visiting the opportunity to feel like royalty for an afternoon or evening. Many of these theaters have remained in operation, and more than a few are said to be home to paranormal activity.

Metropolitan Opera House

Local theaters have often been the subject of ghost stories and tales of roving specters, and Peoria is no exception. The following excerpt was taken from the *Peoria Herald* on August 11, 1869:

The town was excited over the story told by a well-reputed German resident who claimed he had seen a ghost in the ruins of the old Metropolitan Opera House. The man said he was looking into the ruins after dark when the spook came from nowhere and swayed before him. The specter, he said, was clothed in a filmy white garment and flashed two phosphorescent eyes in the darkness. One upper side of his head was missing as though it had been blow off and toward this cavity a bony finger pointed. The German said he was watching the thing, too scared to move, until the creature pointed a skeleton finger at him and vanished. The German said he also vanished from that same place at the same time about as fast as the ghost. Several of the more venturesome souls walked over at night to see if they could locate his ghostship but failed to find him. The next night Tom Phillips sat behind the ruins all night to collect a $10 bet that said he was afraid. The other bettor refused to pay, however, because Phillips kept a shotgun with him which was not in the agreement. Tom argued that he didn't take the gun along with a view of plugging any ghosts, but simply as a precaution against any human beings trying to put a job on him.

The Magnificent Madison Theater
The Madison Theater is located at 502 Main Street, at the northeast corner of Main and Madison Streets in downtown Peoria. The Madison opened to long crowds on October 16, 1920, with the movie *Humoresque*. This was at a time when vaudeville was still the prevalent form of entertainment, but moving motion pictures were growing in popularity. The Madison, as other theaters at that time, began as a silent picture theater and was touted as the "shrine to the silent art." At the time of construction, the theater had a maximum occupancy of 2,000. Ticket prices were 30¢ for matinees and 40¢ for evening pictures. The building was designed by Frederick J. Klein, a Peoria architect.

The front of the theater presents an Italian Renaissance exterior with domed lobby ceilings. There is a triple-arched window above the marquee. The main floor consists of an outer lobby with ticket booth and marquee on Main Street. At the time it was built, the theater was decorated in a tasteful palate of muted gold, cream, and white. The theater seats over 1,600 people in the auditorium and two balconies, with a stage and orchestra pit at the opposite end of the auditorium. The dome of the auditorium consists of concentric circles surrounded by a coved cornice. Underneath the orchestra pit are six dressing rooms, an instrument room, a musician room, and an organist room. At the time of its opening, the Madison featured a 20-piece orchestra to accompany the pictures.

With the advent of talking pictures, the orchestra was no longer necessary to provide the sound for the pictures, and alterations were made to the Madison in 1927, with installation of a $25,000 pipe organ and removal of the orchestra platform. The outer and inner lobbies were remodeled in 1936–1937 with undulating panels and decorative downlights, with an art deco decor tempered by the more moderne style. However, the more ornate features of the theater remained: lunettes, swags, paterae, and Wedgwood-type figures in circular plaques.

The Madison Theater was the stage for many famous vaudeville stars and movie actors during the 1920s and 1930s. The theater was known for its family-friendly fare and had a large child audience. The Madison Theater hosted free Christmas shows for children throughout the 1940s and 1950s. The theater was added to the National Register of Historic Places on November 21, 1980. The Madison closed its doors in 1983 but was later restored and continues to attract crowds for live performances and rock concerts. The theater has also attracted a ghostly following.

The Madison Theater is reportedly home to at least three spirits. The first is that of a young actor who haunts the main stage of the auditorium. He was allegedly killed in the alley next to the theater following his performance, and it is rumored his spirit never left the building. His footsteps can be heard pacing back and forth across the empty stage during times when the theater is deserted, and his presence is often accompanied by the smell of strong cologne. It is reported that this ghost became angry during theater renovations and moved tools brought in by the construction workers in order to try to stop work on the project.

Another ghost is said to lurk in the basement and is allegedly that of a young child who was murdered in the theater in the 1950s after having been lured away from his parents during a show. He appears wearing brown short pants and a white shirt, and his childish laughter has been reported by workers as he darts among the seats of the main auditorium. This ghost is also said to run along one row in a rush of icy-cold air, only to return a few moments later from the opposite direction.

The last ghost at the Madison is that of a former worker at the theater who allegedly haunts the area of the foyer outside the auditorium. His job was to assist in ushering patrons, and the

Here is Madison Theater on opening day in 1920. (Courtesy of the Peoria Public Library, Oakford Collection.)

legend is that the light from his flashlight can still be seen, gliding past the aisles and then disappearing into the darkness.

The Madison Theater remains a bright spot in downtown Peoria and continues to attract those with an interest in live entertainment, theater, or local history. It also continues to be of interest to those with an interest in supernatural activity.

Peoria Players Theater

Peoria Players Theater is the fourth-oldest continuously running community theater in the nation and the oldest in Illinois. The Peoria Players Theater was organized in 1919, when 75 Peorians and amateur thespians met at the home of William Hawley Smith. The next meeting was held at the H. T. Bloom home at 936 North Glen Oak Avenue, and officers were elected.

By the end of its first season, the Peoria Players had produced 16 one-act plays and 1 two-act play. Originally the theater troupe used the women's club stage located in the auxiliary building at the intersection of Fayette and Madison Streets in downtown Peoria. Membership in the theater grew steadily, and by 1928, the membership was over 700. The theater made plans to acquire the old central engine house on Jackson Street for an official theater. The new location was successful, and the membership in the theater grew steadily over the years as larger and more elaborate productions took the stage. Eventually the troupe required yet another move, and the theater at Jackson Street sold on December 31, 1955.

The theater moved to its present location on Lake Street at the new arts and science center in Lakeview Park in 1955. The Peoria Players troupe toured on the road from 1955 to 1956, returning to the Peoria stage for the grand opening of its new theater, held on November 30, 1957.

The Peoria Players Theater provided local direction and talent in its productions, ranging from classic to modern drama. One of these local talents remains quite active in the theater, despite his untimely death. Norman Endean grew up in Peoria and later graduated from Bradley University. Following graduation, Endean lived with his parents and devoted all his free time to the Peoria Players Theater. He became theater manager in the 1950s and directed and acted in a number of plays. Endean loved the local theater and spent most of his spare time rehearsing or reading scripts. In the theater's 39th season from 1957 to 1958, Endean starred in *Ondine* (*Giraudoux*). In the 40th season from 1958 to 1959, he starred in *The Most Happy Fella*. Endean became ill in 1959 while acting in a production of *Kiss Me Kate*, a comedy loosely based on Shakespeare's *Taming of the Shrew*. Endean was admitted to Methodist Hospital on February 14, 1960, and died later that year at 34 years of age. The cause of death was uncertain, but it is reported that he had cancer.

During his tenure as a director at Peoria Players Theater, Norman Endean would sit in the front row of the theater, and from this seat he observed the action and directed. Shortly after his death, theater veterans reported that Endean's spirit had returned to the theater. Endean would appear in a number of ways, turning on and off lights, moving props, and walking backstage. The actors and workers eventually became accustomed to Endean, and he was often used as a scapegoat to explain any problems with a production or set.

Jim Brabowski, a volunteer at Peoria Player Theater for a number of years and former board member, related a number of anecdotes in connection with Norman Endean. Brabowski reported that one afternoon, an employee at the theater brought in his young grandson to do some work in the lighting booth. As the employee was up in the booth, his grandson peered down into the auditorium below. "Granddad, who is that man?" he asked. The man looked up from his work, startled by the question. He knew he and his grandson were alone in the theater. "What man?" He peered down into the seats below, but could not see anyone. "That man, there." The boy pointed to a seat near the back row of the theater. The man looked again but still could not see anyone there. The boy later described to his grandfather that a man dressed in a light gray suit

Norman Endean's ghost is said to haunt Peoria Players Theater. (Courtesy of the Peoria Players Theater.)

The makeup room at Peoria Players Theater is one of many areas where actors have reported encountering the ghost of Norman Endean.

Norman Endean will often watch performances from the catwalk.

had been sitting at the back of theater, watching the stage. The man sat there while the man and his grandson were in the lighting booth, and then he had disappeared. The man searched the theater, which only confirmed that he and his grandson were alone. He decided it was time to wrap up for the day and hastily left the theater.

On another occasion, a veteran actress was giving a performance center stage when she happened to look up to her left. Standing there on the highest catwalk was a man watching the performance. She looked at him and felt a sudden chill. She knew she was looking at the ghost of Norman Endean. She reported that he watched the performance a few seconds, and when she next looked up at the catwalk, he had disappeared.

Jim Brabowski related that during a recent performance of *Annie Get Your Gun*, Endean was particularly active. His favorite activity was moving the stacks of lumber at the back of the stage that were being used to build props for the old frontier town. The administrators and workers frequently heard the sound of these lumber piles being moved, but upon investigation, nothing appeared to have been touched backstage.

Norman Endean does not seem particularly enthused by his notoriety, resisting entreaties and demands to show himself or act on command. A former patron of the theater was going through the belongings of a local elderly woman and came across a picture of Norman Endean and the playbill from *Kiss Me Kate*. The woman was the former girlfriend of Endean and had carefully preserved the few mementos of her past love. The theater is now in possession of these artifacts. Interestingly, a large photograph of Endean that was recovered was placed in the costume area. The large, poster-size photograph subsequently disappeared from the theater. It is believed that the ghost of Norman Endean, never one for publicity, had taken the matter into his own hands and moved the picture from the common area.

If the ghost of Norman Endean is at the theater, he is a protective and sometimes mischievous presence. Endean is affectionately regarded by the actors and staff and has been given a welcoming home by those familiar with the theater.

Peoria Players Theater continues to play host to a variety of productions, highlighting the talents of various local actors and providing top-quality art and entertainment for the city. When visiting, make sure to send out a silent "hello" to Endean; he will be sitting in one of the rows at the back, getting ready for the next show.

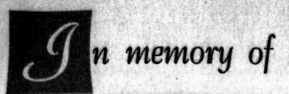

In memory of

our beloved

Norman D. Endean

born

March _12_ _1926_
month   day   year

birthplace

Peoria, _Illinois_
town   state

Peoria, Illinois _February 29, 196_
place of death   date

age

_34_ _11_ _17_
years   months   days

Here is the memory book from Norman Endean's 1960 funeral. (Courtesy of the Peoria Players Theater.)

Two

MADNESS

Oh, that way madness lies; let me shun that.
                    —William Shakespeare, *King Lear*, act 3, scene 4

Bartonville State Mental Hospital

If a visitor followed U.S. Route 24 south through the city of Peoria and into Bartonville around a hill overlooking the wooded edge of the Illinois River bluff, they might be surprised at the sight of a towering and decrepit three-story stone structure at the top of the hill. The broken and boarded windows convey a sense of desolation and loss. The stranger visiting would be hard-pressed to give an explanation for this building. An old university? A medical building? What they would be looking at are the remains of a revolution in the treatment of the mentally ill—a vast, sprawling institution that at its height was the home of some 4,000 asylum inmates. And, if rumor is any indication, continues to be the home of many of those same spirits.

The Peoria State Hospital Historic District occupies this site today. It is a complex of 47 buildings, 33 of which were part of the original hospital constructed between 1899 and 1910. Inmates from all over the state of Illinois were shipped to this mental health community via railroad and escorted from the train tracks up a long wooden staircase to the doors of the insane asylum. Once they arrived, they were classified according to the level of aberrant behavior, stripped, and showered. They were then wrapped in layers of wet sheets and placed in bed in order to calm them. They were sometimes left in that manner for a number of days, depending on the degree of lunacy observed.

This system would change drastically with the entry of Dr. George Zeller into the mental health arena. Dr. Zeller was born in 1858 in Spring Bay and graduated from the University of Illinois in 1876 and from St. Louis Medical College in 1879. He practiced medicine in Spring Bay until 1889, when he married and traveled to Europe where he studied the European methods of care and compassionate treatment of the insane. In 1890, he returned to Peoria and opened an office on Main Street opposite the site of the former Peoria courthouse. He was instrumental in changing the adjudication of insanity cases in Peoria.

In the late 1880s in the Peoria area, an insanity inquiry (*de lunatico inquirendo*) was perfunctory at best. A writ was issued commanding the person who had custody of the person alleged to be insane produce them before the court. The inquiry itself consisted of a single printed form on which the finding was written and signed by the jury. There was no background medical information or social history to forward to asylum officials to ensure proper treatment. The single-form insanity inquiry was revised by state committee in consultation with Dr. Zeller. The resultant form contained a comprehensive family, social, and professional history of the patient. In addition, the law required examination of insane suspects by two medical experts. With the help of visionaries such as Dr. Zeller, eventually the idea of public and private mental hospitals replaced the poorhouse and prison. In the late 1880s, a group of Peoria women, headed by the president of the Peoria Women's Club, Clara Parsons Bourland, formed an organization to procure funds for the establishment of a facility for the incurably insane. In 1895, the Illinois

Here is the stately Bowen Building of Peoria State Hospital.

state legislature granted the group $65,000 for this purpose. The people of Bartonville donated 318 acres of land for the construction of this institution.

The Illinois Asylum for the Incurable Insane opened on February 10, 1902, receiving 100 patients from the Illinois State Hospital in Jacksonville. In November 1902, Dr. George Zeller began his tenure as superintendent of the hospital. Dr. Zeller noted that if anyone treated a dog or horse as cruelly as the insane they would be brought into court. He noted in the fifth biennial report of 1904, "Nothing in my mind emphasized the necessity of an institution of this kind as a study of the cases brought to us. Many were old and feeble, some had spent more than 40 years in almshouses, a number were blind or had lost a limb. Complete imbecility was common."

The population of the hospital grew steadily as patients were transferred from poorhouse to hospital. By June 30, 1906, there were 1,729 residents; by 1907, there were 2,008; and by 1908, 2,221 patients called this place home. The average age of an inmate was 47, and the age at death was 57. By 1909, the term *asylum* changed to *state hospital*, the term *inmate* to *patient*, and the term *poorhouse* to *county home*. As quickly as buildings were constructed they were filled by insane individuals from every county in the state.

Early asylum inmates were not considered sick but rather animalistic. Therefore there was no need to protect such people or even consider basic human needs such as clothing and shelter. Their ability to endure extreme temperatures with inadequate cover confirmed that these individuals were not people at all. The animalistic nature of these individuals was thought only curable by discipline and brutal aggression.

In order to cure mania and melancholia, a number of bizarre theories and treatments emerged. One of these involved the desolation of fermentations in the mind that enslaved the individual. This involved the consumption of coffee, quinine, chimney soot, soap, soluble tartar, honey, wood lice, powdered lobster claw, or bezoar. Another theory was that of purification, wherein areas of the body were centers of evacuation of the bad humor. This was accomplished by provoking open sores and then burning and cauterizing the area. The victims were subjected to the introduction of scabies, eczema, or smallpox that would cause open sores through which the bad humors could escape.

A popular cure with surprising long-term utilization has been immersion, in which hot or cold water was used to cure either mania or depression. In a "shower proper," the individual was fastened to an armchair that was placed beneath a reservoir filled with cold water, while a large pipe poured cold water directly to the head. Another such method was the "surprise bath," where the individual would be pushed unexpectedly from a ledge into a large pool of water.

In 1934, convulsive therapy was used to induce seizure activity. These were electrically induced currents, and patients would often break bones in their writhing and convulsions. The first controlled human lobotomy was performed in 1936 and consisted of drilling holes into the patient's head and destroying the brain tissue with alcohol injections. In later performed transorbital lobotomies, a mallet was used to force an ice pick through the skull at the top of the eye socket, and then the front lobe was scrambled to produce the desired effect.

The lives of many of those languishing in asylums were often cut short by these attempts to "cure" them. Sometimes these cures were the results of good intentions; but often the inmates died from either neglect or deliberate cruelty. It is little wonder that asylums throughout the United States have surfaced as some of the most haunted sites in the country. The poor wretches who found no peace in life seemed condemned in many cases to remain at the site of their ofttimes violent demise.

Dr. Zeller sought to bring a new approach to the treatment of the mentally ill, and the Illinois Asylum for the Incurable Insane was established as a "cottage system" with 33 different buildings, including a nurses' home, a store, a bakery, and a kitchen. Many of the remains of these buildings can still be found today on the hospital grounds. In addition to the many outbuildings, there was a farm where inmates could find vocation. There were also four cemeteries that are still in existence today.

Even with these progressive reforms there were reports of abuse and unexplained deaths. During various times in the hospital's history, there was at least one death per day. Dr. Zeller attributed this in large part to former staffers who were less educated regarding treatment reform and kept to the "old ways" of treatment.

The first fatality from abuse took place on October 19, 1903, with the death of Thomas H. He was reportedly beaten to death by two attendants, although neither man was indicted for his death. The coroner testimony was graphic, describing horrific bruising on the neck and trunk from a club or heavy boot. The back and stomach were beaten beyond recognition, destroying his inner organs. Thomas H. lived for three hours after this beating. There was no mention of the fate of the two attendants, but it is doubtful they faced any criminal prosecution.

Although Dr. Zeller noted his institution contained "the most violent, destructive, and habitually untidy patients of any in the state," he remained dedicated to a system of nonrestraint. As mentioned earlier, Dr. Zeller removed all restraints formerly used, including leather anklets, wristlets, and bed saddles. By November 1, 1905, Dr. Zeller reported that there were 2,000 patients at the hospital without a bar on any window, a locked room, or any mechanical or medicinal restraints.

Rest and humane treatment were Dr. Zeller's preferred methods of treatment, and he advanced his cause in unique and innovative ways. Dr. Zeller took the $6,000 worth of old iron grates and created a zoo on the premises. The zoo was a source of amusement and delight to patients, visitors, and attendants. Concrete dens and caves were created along with watering holes. By 1910, there were 13 deer in the deer park, along with coyotes and foxes. A young black bear from Washington State had been trained to take a bath on command. Hundreds of visitors to the zoo noted the grating and marveled that it was once used to cage humans. The following story regarding the zoo appeared in the *Peoria Herald Transcript* in June 1913:

> One of the queerest freaks of fate to be displayed to the human race is to be found in the grounds of the Peoria State Hospital for the Insane at Bartonville. Here is the only institution for insane in the world where bolts, locks, and bars are not used nor known by the inmates insane or declared so by commissions and thereby worthy of imprisonment or restraint, are building a zoo for the caging of wild animals, and every grate, bar, chain and lock in the construction of the cages and pens has at some time in the past served to cage human beings. Such is the mockery of fate. The main corral, around an acreage of sufficient size to farm and in which are all cages and the pens, is made from the iron-barred grates which were taken from the doors of the same hospital when Dr. George A. Zeller, the present superintendent, took charge several years ago. There are scores of these "strong doors" made into one endless fence about the zoo.

Patients were provided with adequate food and pleasant surroundings. Restraints were only used as a last resort on the most unruly of patients. Various activities such as reading, gardening, and playing games were encouraged and readily available. This humane treatment led to a level of camaraderie among the patients. Dr. Zeller noted that they had become highly efficient at caring for one another, and if one fell the others would immediately provide on-the-spot care.

Dr. Zeller, an advocate of color therapy, built a black room for treatment of the extremely violent patients. This room had a black floor, black bed, black walls, and black curtains. Although the room usually remained in total darkness, Dr. Zeller noted in the summer the windows would need to be opened to avoid excessive heat. One particularly violent patient was placed in the black room. She fell asleep, and in three days was able to return to her cottage greatly improved. It was noted to be especially useful in the treatment of "hysterical insanity," and those given the cure generally improved.

Although it was decreasing in popularity, trephining (or trepanation) was still in practice at the hospital. This is a form of surgery in which a hole is drilled or scraped into the skull, thus exposing the brain matter and supposedly relieving pressure on the brain. Dr. Zeller noted that nine cases of dementia paralysis were treated with trephining of the skull. Only one of the patients survived this treatment. It should not be presumed that Dr. Zeller was engaged in antiquated or tortuous methods of treatment, these were the most accepted treatments at the time and were implemented in an effort to help improve the lives of the patients, not in an attempt to exploit their condition. Dr. Zeller brought innovative methods in mental health treatment and saved many lives. During his tenure, the mortality rates of the patients dropped dramatically. For many, duration of insanity was less than one month.

Perhaps in acknowledgement of the possibility of improvement, the Illinois legislature changed the name in 1907 to the Illinois General Hospital for the Insane and in 1909 changed the name to Peoria State Hospital.

Dr. Zeller was active in community and civic affairs and had a keen interest in Peoria history. He bought Jubilee College and grounds in 1933 and donated the grounds to the State of Illinois for a park. His wife later donated the chapel. Dr. Zeller retired in 1935, and he and his wife continued to live at their residence on the grounds of the Peoria State Hospital. Dr. Zeller died on June 29, 1939, at the age of 80, and his funeral was held at the Peoria State Hospital attended by friends, family, dignitaries, and former and present patients. Dr. Zeller was buried next to his wife on Vista Hill in Springdale Cemetery.

Social "Reform" and the Demise of the Institution

The Illinois Asylum for the Incurable Insane had at its peak 3,000 patients in the early 1950s. The population of the institution began to decline after the discovery of new antidepressant drugs, which allowed many of those previously relegated to asylum care free to pursue outpatient treatment. In addition, public sentiment favored the theory that psychiatric hospitals were merely overcrowded, filthy prisons more focused on torturing society's nonconformists than curing mental illness. "Institutional dependency" became a popular sociological concept. In his novel *One Flew Over the Cuckoo's Nest*, author Ken Kesey described a tyrannical, sadistic medical staff devoted to forcing the patients into total submission by whatever means possible. Despite studies that showed patients at state hospitals were free to leave at any time, there was a general feeling that these institutions oppressed and imprisoned the patients.

In the late 1960s, reform laws prevented patients from working at the institution. This led to increased budgets and patient idleness. The activities that had given these poor individuals a sense of place and accomplishment were forbidden to them. Many patients would hopefully return to their duty stations on a daily basis, seeking the solace and comfort of work activity and sense of well-being occasioned by the opportunity to assist the community. By mid-1960, Peoria State Hospital established a mental retardation unit. Mental health treatment shifted from a pastoral community "cure-all" lasting decades to a quick-turnaround open-door treatment.

By 1965, the population of the Peoria State Hospital was at 2,300; by the time of the hospital's close in 1973, there were only 280 patients remaining. Only five buildings were in use at that time, and the hospital had become a nursing home. A report from the Illinois Investigating Commission on December 18, 1973, reported the shocking condition of the buildings and remaining patients. The buildings were filthy and in a state of decay and disrepair. The odors of urine and excrement filled the halls. There were excrement smears on virtually every wall. The patients wandered the halls in torn, dirty clothing or in no clothing whatsoever. Many of the patients were filthy and had open sores or untreated illness. The heavy use of narcotics kept the mentally retarded in a state of constant stupor. Overmedication slowed all forms of treatment, including physical and occupational therapy since the patients were slow to respond and could not remember skills.

In 1972, two mentally retarded patients were murdered and a third died from meningitis. Jerome S. was beaten to death on May 21, 1972, apparently by another patient. He had been repeatedly beaten on several occasions prior to his death. Bernard R. was struck in the head by a fellow patient on July 19, 1972, and did not receive treatment until the following day. He died as a result of these injuries. James L. had a history of ear infection and was the victim of medical neglect. He died on August 29, 1972, from spinal meningitis occasioned by his ear infection. These deaths, combined with the aforementioned commission findings, led to the closing of the state hospital in 1973. By December 18 of that year, the last 18 patients were transferred to the Galesburg State Research Hospital.

In 1986, the City of Bartonville acquired the hospital land with the intention of development into an industrial park. All the original buildings that formed the integral part of the hospital complex, although intact, are in various stages of decay, disrepair, and in some cases, collapse.

The public is likely to lose the historical places where Dr. George Zeller carried out his innovative treatments. Without more public or civic interest, the buildings will ultimately need to be razed, and the entire state will lose the ability to observe a stronghold of forward-thinking mental health treatment. It is unclear what fate awaits those buried in the cemeteries on the grounds, and such uncertainty undoubtedly adds to the restlessness of some of those troubled souls.

Old Book and the Graveyard Elm

The following is an excerpt from *Asylum Light*, Volume 2, No. 3 (December 1937), a monthly newsletter published by the Peoria State Hospital:

> When the governor placed me in charge of the big new asylum for the insane that the state had just erected, I recognized that along with the problem of the living, the disposal of the dead was one that must also have its share of attention.
>
> We buried the bodies of the friendless and unclaimed, as the remains of the well-to-do were shipped at the expense of the friends and relatives to such points as they designated. As the rows of headstones multiplied and extended, our cemetery became an object of interest and the impressive service that marked each funeral were largely attended.
>
> The burial corps consisted of a reliable employee and a half dozen insane men who were handy with the spade and who went mechanically through the process of digging a grave and just as mechanically refilled it after the coffin had been lowered.

With over 2,000 inmates, mostly elderly and indigent, the hospital's high death rate was nearly matched by the number of deceased left to it for burial. This kept the grave diggers busy. The hospital housed many "interesting characters," and most unique of all was one A. Bookbinder. Sent to Peoria State Hospital from a local poorhouse and unable to speak coherently, all that was known about this man was that he had worked in a printing house, "a book binder," according to the officer who took him in once the mental aberration manifested itself. He expressed himself only in writing, and except for official records this individual was named by all simply as "Old Book."

> He was strong and healthy, considerably demented but harmless, and the attendants were not long in finding him a desirable worker and in time he became a member of the funeral

Peoria State Hospital Cemetery is the final resting place of hundreds of mad souls.

Here is the famous "Old Elm" at Peoria State Hospital.

corps. He developed a strong interesting trait at the first funeral in which he participated. Ordinarily when the coffin was being lowered the shovelers stood back, silently awaiting the end of the ceremony, when they would lay to with vigor and complete the interment. The dead were all strangers to us and our ceremony was simply a mark of respect rather than an indication of personal attachment to the deceased. Therefore, it may be imagined how surprised we were when, at the critical moment, Old Book removed his cap, began to wipe his eyes and finally give vent to loud lamentations. The first few times he did this emotion become contagious and there were many moist eyes at the graveside, but when at each succeeding burial his feeling overcame him and it was realized that Book was possessed of a mania that manifested itself in an uncontrollable grief.

Those of us who had studied association tests could see in this symptom the revival of some great crisis through which he had passed, some might sorrow he had experienced and which in itself might have been the cause of the dethronement of his reason.

Old Book had no favorites, and his routine never varied when mourning the dead.

At the psychological moment he would step back, spade in hand, in an attitude of waiting. First his left and then his right sleeve would be raised to wipe away a furtive tear but as the coffin began to descend into the grave he would walk over and lean against the big elm that stood in the center of the lot and give vent to sobs that convulsed his frame and which could be heard by the entire assemblage.

This particular tree was a magnificent specimen of *Ulmas Americana*, or spreading elm. It dwarfed surrounding trees, casting its shadow across the whole area, its "generous branches afford[ing] shelter to hundreds of patients" from the hot summer sun. Known as "the Graveyard Elm," it became the most photographed tree on the premises, often appearing in annual reports as the physical symbol for the institution's motto: "Sane Surroundings for the Insane."

The infirmities of age and intercurrent disease continued to deplete our population about as fast as it was recruited. We were singularly free from epidemics and even from fatal accidents, but the average age of our inmates was fifty-eight years and we could not stay the hands of Father Time. The only exercise that "Old Book" took consisted of attending funerals. His long association with these functions had made him a fixture and a funeral would not have been considered complete without his presence.

Indeed, hospital employees grew to respect Old Book and his mania. Nurses kept him posted of upcoming funerals and dressed him appropriately for wind, rain, or shine. No burial seemed complete without his outbursts of grief.

In the natural order of events it came Book's turn to be carried to his last resting place and, as might be inferred, this was an event that excited more than usual interest. The news spread rapidly that "Book" had shed his last teat and through that quick process by which word passes among the employees of an institution, it was agreed that they attend his funeral in a body.

It was an impressive sight. The hour was set for noon on a beautiful June day, a time that permitted the greatest attendance, and everyone came. Over against the hillside more than a hundred uniformed nurses were grouped like a great bank of white lilies while around the grave stood the staff and a large force of men, together with several hundred privileged patients. As was not infrequently the case, I officiated in person. The coffin rested upon two cross beams over the open grave and four sturdy men stood ready to man the ropes by which it was to be lowered. Just as the choir finished the last line of "Rock of Ages" the men grasped the ropes, stooped forward, and with a powerful muscular effort prepared to lift the coffin in order to permit the removal of the crossbeams and allow it gently descend into the grave.

At a given signal they heaved away at the ropes and the next instant all four lay prone on their backs; for the coffin, instead of offering resistance, bounded into the air like an eggshell as if it were empty.

This caused much consternation as the nurses shrieked, half of them fleeing the scene. Above all the noise and confusion, however, was heard by all "a wailing voice," turning all eyes to the great elm tree from which the cry emanated.

Every man and woman stood transfixed, for there, just as had always been the case, stood "Old Book" weeping and moaning with an earnestness that outrivaled anything he had ever shown before.

We could not be mistaken. It was the same "Old Book" and there was the same old cloth cap and the same handkerchief around the neck, and the attitude with which we were all familiar.

I am not superstitious, and continuous association with the insane had long ago taught me to avoid psychic contamination, therefore I, in common with the other bystanders, stood transfixed at the sight of this apparition. There stood the nurses who were at his bedside when he died, there was the undertaker who had embalmed his body and the six men who as pallbearers had carried the heavy coffin from the hearse and placed it over the grave, yet there in plain sight and in the attitude so familiar to all of us stood "Book". Even though he had been invisible his lamentations would have been sufficient to identify him. It was broad daylight and there could be no deception. No one moved or spoke and a paralytic fear came over us.

Summoning courage, several helpers removed the coffin lid, hands trembling as they loosened screws.

I nerved myself to step forward in order to peer into the empty coffin but just as they lifted the lid the wailing sound ceased and at the identical moment we gazed upon the calm features of our old mourner. There he lay, cold in death dressed in his somber shroud with his hands folded across his breast. Everybody was invited to file by and identify the remains but it was noticed that after casting a glance at the corpse every eye wandered over to the old elm. The tree stood there in all its stateliness—the apparition had vanished—and the funeral was completed as if it had not suffered this uncanny interruption except that many were weeping through the delayed ceremony.

Three hundred spectators were witness to this ghastly event. And within a few weeks, the groundskeeper reported that the Graveyard Elm had begun to whither, leaves shriveling despite bucket after bucket of water poured about its roots.

There was nothing to do and in a few weeks it was bare of leaves and by late fall many of its lesser twigs had fallen. In the course of time other branches dropped until finally only the main stem and large forks remained. There it stood plainly outlined against the sky, a monarch of the forest still, in spite of its absence of life. On a moonlight night its giant arms resembled those of a human skeleton and it came to be looked upon with a feeling of awe and dread, yet no one was willing to undertake the task of cutting it down.

One of our men tried it but at the first stroke he threw down his axe and ran to his quarters declaring that in the clouds of smoke that curved upward he could plainly outline the features of our departed mourner.

There is one unmarked grave in the cemetery and when visitors comment on the missing monument the guide hastily changes the subject and points with a shudder to the Graveyard Elm.

The Witchcraft of Rhoda Derry

Rhoda Derry was brought to the Illinois State Asylum in 1904. At that time, the population of the hospital was growing rapidly, to the extent that there were approximately 200 new patients per month admitted. One night in the autumn of that year, a train car arriving from Quincy was late and did not arrive at the hospital until 1:00 a.m. The exhausted hospital personnel had been admitting patients since early that morning and wearily set out to the railroad crossing to meet the latest group of patients. As the group was led from the car, one of the railroad men handed down a clothes basket, which was taken along with the new patients up to the top of the hill. It was believed the basket contained the effects of the newly arrived patients, so the group was very surprised when the basket began to move and a strange language was heard. Uncovering the cloth on top of the basket, the nurses beheld a strange sight.

Rhoda Derry had been placed in the local county house in Quincy at the age of 22 or 23 and had lived in institutions for 43 years. After her hospitalization, Derry lost the ability to walk upright. As a result, she ambulated by using her arms and balled fists to propel herself around. Rhoda's body was contorted, and her knees rested against her chest. She refused to wear clothing and was often kept tied to a bed or chair to prevent her from wandering the halls naked. Derry slept in a Utica bed, a criblike bed with a top that would effectively hold a person. The bed was lined with straw that was changed periodically as Derry soiled her bed. Derry was subject to occasional violent episodes and would beat herself and others in her vicinity. During one such spell, she gauged out her own eyes and was blinded. She would eat with her hands and would put anything in her mouth that she came in contact with. Derry never received a formal diagnosis for her mental health problems. Many of her neighbors believed she had been bewitched by a jealous woman after a failed love affair and that her malady was attributable to witchcraft.

Rhoda Derry was 66 when she came to the Illinois State Asylum, and she quickly became the object of sympathetic interest to the nursing staff and was treated as a favored child. When the weather was nice, the nurses would put her on a mattress and set her on one of the porches. Derry died in October 1906 at age 68. Soon after her death, there were reports that Derry's spirit had not left the beloved institution. The nurses would frequently report seeing her sitting on the sun porch just as she had done in life. Derry is buried in grave 217 at the asylum cemetery. Her grave is clearly marked and can be visited to this day.

The Reincarnation of Mary Roff

Mary Roff was born in Indiana in October 1846. As a young girl, she suffered from seizure activity, which intensified as she got older. Mary also suffered from auditory hallucinations and trancelike states where she would remain unresponsive. Mary claimed to be possessed by the spirits of several different people. She became increasingly convinced that her blood was tainted and began to experiment with different methods of removing her blood, including cutting and the use of leaches. Mary eventually tried to commit suicide by slashing her wrists. Mary's parents had her committed to the Illinois State Asylum in Bartonville before her 18th birthday. During her time there, she was subject to immersion treatment, in which ice-cold and hot water were

217

RHODA DERRY

1840 - 1906

THEY BUILT THIS PLACE OF ASYLUM SO THAT NO
OTHER HUMAN WOULD SUFFER AS YOU.
YOU TAUGHT US TO LOVE AND FEEL
COMPASSION TOWARDS THE LESS FORTUNATE.

MAY YOU FIND PEACE AND WARMTH IN GOD'S ARMS.

Here is the grave site of Rhoda Derry, said to still haunt the grounds of the abandoned institution.

used alternatively. She was also subject to numerous cleansings through the use of douches and wrappings in icy-cold sheets, both methods believed to improve circulation. Mary spent the rest of her short life at the asylum and died on July 5, 1865.

The tragic story might have ended there, if not for the experience of a young girl from Watseka named Lurancy Vennum. Lurancy was born on April 16, 1864, the year before Mary Roff died. Like Mary, Lurancy was plagued by mental problems and in her early teens began to experience the same trancelike states that had afflicted Mary. During her trances, Lurancy would assume different personalities and voices. On one such occasion in 1877, Lurancy fell into a coma, and was unconscious for five hours. When she could finally be roused, she remembered nothing of the event. She told her family that during these spells she could speak with other spirits and hear voices of the departed. After this episode, the trances began to occur more regularly. Lurancy would speak in strange, nonsensical languages and upon wakening would remember nothing from these episodes. The tales of Lurancy Vennum and her strange affliction began to circulate about the area and were included in a story in the local newspaper.

The Vennum family had never heard of the Roff family or Mary Roff until 1878, when Mary's father, Asa Roff, came to visit with Lurancy. He had heard tales of her hallucinations and trances and was struck by their resemblance to those that had plagued his own daughter, Mary. He believed the spirit of his daughter Mary might be within the 14-year-old Lurancy Vennum. Lurancy's minister and physician had recommended to her parents that she be sent to the Illinois Asylum for the Incurable Insane for treatment. Asa Roff sought to intervene. He did not believe the treatment his daughter Mary had received had cured her and believed that her death had been preventable. During his visit with the Vennum family, Asa Roff was accompanied by Dr. E. Winchester, a noted spiritualist. Dr. Winchester used hypnosis on Lurancy, and under this spell Lurancy spoke as many different spirits who inhabited her body.

Eventually the spirit of Mary Roff appeared. The trance continued until the next day, and by the time she was roused by Dr. Winchester, Lurancy Vennum believed she had become Mary Roff. She told her family she wanted to go back home with Asa Roff. She did not recognize the Vennum house or the Vennum family. However, Lurancy knew everything about the Roff family and asked questions revealing intimate details about the Roffs that the Vennum family could not possibly know. Lurancy was pleasant but distant with her own family but very familiar and warm toward the Roffs. The Vennums were understandably resistant to the idea of their daughter going to a different family, but finally on February 11, 1878, she was allowed to go for visit with the Roff family. As time passed, the personality of Lurancy almost completely disappeared as she held all the memories and experiences of Mary Roff. She had almost forgotten both Lurancy Vennum and the Vennum family. She did not recall family members, friends, or events from her old life.

Despite her claims that the Vennums were now strangers to her, the Vennum family continued to visit Lurancy in the hopes her old identity would reassert itself. Lurancy/Mary's physical condition improved dramatically during her stay, and she no longer experienced the trances and hallucinations that had defined her adolescence. In May, Lurancy/Mary told the Roff family that she had to leave them and became increasingly despondent and upset. Mary disappeared a short time later, and Lurancy returned home to the Vennums. She seemed to have completely recovered from whatever mental illness had plagued her adolescence and remained happy and healthy.

Lurancy married a local farmer and moved to Kentucky. They had 11 children together, and Lurancy did not have any mental health problems until her death in the late 1940s. Mary Roff never reappeared; her second life seemingly ended in 1878, 13 years after her mortal death.

Bartonville and Its Aftermath

Ghosts and insanity have often gone hand-in-hand, as many manifestations of insanity involve seeing or hearing what to most is not there. There are many reasons attributed to the presence of these ghosts: they want to replay their death, comfort the living, or right a wrong. Most commonly mentioned in fiction is the unfinished business of a proper burial. This might explain the many stories of haunting on the grounds of the old state hospital. Local folklore maintains that a spirit will linger near the body for many years, either to warn the living or due to an inability to move on to another plane. Whatever the case, there appears to be a high level of such activity at this site.

When the hospital closed in 1973, there were 4,132 patients buried in the asylum's four cemeteries, most in unmarked graves in cemeteries 1 and 2. Dr. George Zeller developed a numbering system for his cemeteries, and that system and the names made part of it have never been publicly disclosed. It is unclear why Dr. Zeller chose a number system instead of using personal inscriptions, but such a system was undoubtedly cheaper. Dr. Zeller took pride that each burial was accompanied by a short service, and the dead were always carried to the cemetery feet forward.

With so many burials, it really is no wonder that such a wide array of ghosts have been reported on the grounds. There are rumors that many of these graves are actually empty, and that the graves were excavated soon after the funeral in order for the bodies to be sent for medical research. There is no recorded history of such events, but the rumors persist to this day.

There have been sightings of mysterious figures in the cemeteries, including the restless and bereaved Old Book. Many have said that if one goes to the cemetery where Old Book was laid to rest on a peaceful summer day, his spirit will appear, wailing and bereaving the loss of one of his fallen comrades, appearing just as he did before the astonished group of the asylum so many years ago. The legend persists that the limbs and branches of the old elm will shake with the force of the sobbing.

There also persist rumors of a so-called "secret cemetery" where those who died from abuse, neglect, or medical experimentation were interred. However, these rumors greatly discredit Dr. Zeller, since presumptively he would have been in collusion with those who sought to hide these atrocities and would have been required to authorize such a scheme. Even in the research for this story, the author encountered rumors of cemeteries in addition to the four on the grounds that have simply been washed away in the ravines that surround this area. Those poor souls have no ultimate resting place and contribute to the mournful atmosphere of the cemetery grounds.

Even before the hospital closed its doors, rumors began to surface of disturbing sights and sounds inside the hospital buildings. There were reports of strange lights and green orbs flitting past windows. There were sounds of doors that would open and close of their own volition. There are legends of underground tunnels that run to the nearby railroad that were once used for supplies, or as some more sensationally suggest, a convenient way to dispose of the violently insane arrivals.

Many visiting the state hospital have been impressed by the distinctively restless impression on the grounds, a deep and forlorn sadness permeating the earth. For many patients, this was home. The most common experience of visitors seems to be moving shadows or "shadow people." These are shadows that appear to have some substance—able to "walk" across doorways and block some light. These are usually accompanied by an icy blast of freezing air. These are malevolent entities, doomed to restlessly wander the grounds and relive the last moments of their untimely, and ofttimes violent deaths.

One of the most popular ghosts is "the Shadow Man" who walks the corridors of the Bowen Building. One source reported that she and her friends visited the Bowen Building in high school. As they were walking down the hallway on the main floor, they had a very strange feeling that they were being watched from the shadows. She described that the hair on the back of their necks stood up and they stopped talking and laughing. They stopped in the middle of the hallway to try to figure out if someone else was in the building. They called out and asked

Apparitions of a nurse have been seen appearing in this second-story window.

whoever was there to come out of the darkness and stop trying to scare them. The only response was a rush of cold air from one of the back rooms. That was enough for the group, and they turned and headed toward the exit. The group started to run, pushing each other in their haste to get away from whatever was pursuing them. When she finally got to the door, the woman reported that she looked back and saw an immense shadow shape emerge from the wall and melt into a room opposite. At the same time, she reported an overwhelming sense of sadness and doom. She said she had never felt that kind of sadness before and has never felt it since. She and her friends kept running back to their car. As they drove away, she kept a careful eye on the old hospital, willing whatever was inside to stay there and not follow her. She reported that she has never gone back to the hospital since that time and was still afraid, even years later, that whatever had seen her before would somehow remember who she was and decide to stay with her. Some say this entity is one of those poor unfortunates like Jerome S. who met a violent and untimely end in the grounds of the old state hospital.

In addition to the Shadow Man, glowing orbs or so-called "spirit orbs" have also been photographed at the hospital. These small balls of light appear almost like lightbulbs or specks of dust when captured on film and are often reported to fly around corridors and create other orbs. A group investigating the alleged hauntings stayed overnight at the Bowen Building in 1998. They reported experiencing cold spots in the basement, as well as encountering two green orbs of former orderlies dubbed "Ed" and "Al." The group also reported hearing thumps and howls and noted a white transparent glow in a stairwell.

There are also rumors of the presence of children on the grounds. One source reported hearing the sounds of small feet running through the halls during a late-night visit. Sometimes these sounds are accompanied by childish laughter or singing. It is of note that many children of those working at the hospital also lived on the grounds. In addition, there are records that some of the female inmates gave birth to children during their stay, and some of those children were adopted by hospital employees. In any case, the hospital was home to many children over the years, and it is entirely possible that some of those 4,000 graves contain the remains of children who lived and died at the asylum.

Another more disturbing sighting involves the observation of "devil eyes" at the windows or in the hallways of the Bowen Building. Many visiting this place at night have reported the sight of a pair of red, glowing eyes burning through the pitch-black darkness. It is possible there might be wild animals inside the buildings, but this does not lessen the impact of these accounts. These are also consistent with the stories of those feeling watched or hunted within the halls. These stories are consistent with other accounts that if people drive by in the moonlight, they will be able to see ghostly faces looking back out of the window, watching as they pass.

Stories of this kind linger at the old state hospital where those who lie in unmarked graves will never have their story told. Society puts much emphasis on a proper burial and the observation of sacred rights that affirm the impact the dead had on the living and show respect for the sanctity of life. There are no biographies in existence of those that marked their time here, no family stories handed down through generations. These were truly the bereft and the forgotten. The only remaining testament to these lives—to the thoughts, passions, ideas, friendships, and fears of thousands of souls—is a number in a row of unkempt graves. Restless? Perhaps with reason. Few would care to end up in an unmarked grave.

Bowen Today

The author recently took a tour of the Bowen Building and part of the hospital grounds. Christina Morris, the historian for the Save the Bowen organization, shared many facts and personal anecdotes during the tour. She frequently leads groups through the Bowen Building and is well informed in the history of the area and of the hospital.

Peoria's Haunted Memories

The Bowen Building was built in 1929 for dormitory residences and administrative offices. In front of the Bowen Building a sunken garden was installed as a recreation area for the patients and staff. The indentation of the garden remains, although a warehouse is presently located at the site.

Upon entering the Bowen Building, Morris related that during the tenure of Dr. George Zeller the first floor of the building consisted of administrative offices. According to Morris, there is one ghost named Sharon who frequently appears at the north end of the administrative hallway. She appears to both visitors and workers and has been described as a young girl in a white hospital gown, with her hair worn in two long braids. It is believed by those familiar with the hospital that Sharon is the ghost of a former patient. She is a protective presence at the hospital and appears to assist when someone is upset or when more malevolent spirits might be present.

The second floor of the Bowen Building contains patient rooms, nurses' dormitory rooms, and communal areas. At the far north end, over 120 women lived and worked within the hospital. These women, like all other patients, had free range of the hospital and grounds. Sadly, many of the women that were sent to the hospital were pregnant, with no one willing to come forward to claim the child. At that time, insanity, and even mental retardation, were considered by many to be hereditary diseases, and few were willing to risk raising such a child as their own. The women were allowed to keep their children until the age of four, at which time they became wards of the state. Many of the nurses who cared for these women later adopted the children and raised them on the hospital grounds. Many electronic voice phenomenon, or EVPs, have been reported in the women's dormitory, with the voices of women and children laughing and talking most prominently heard. A doll is kept at the north end of the corridor for the amusement of these ghost children.

The second floor also contained classrooms and work areas at the south end. In one of these classrooms, the apparition of a nurse appears to visitors and workers. The nurse wears the long, formal gown required by Dr. Zeller, along with the requisite crisp full-length apron. Her hair is dressed befitting the period, worn in a high bun in the Gibson-girl style popular in the early 1900s. During one visit, a tourist was outside taking pictures of the second floor of the Bowen from the back of the building. She captured on her film what appeared to be the apparition of a woman. A closer review of the film revealed a full-body apparition in a gown of the early 20th century with the hair arranged in a bun. The figure was completely transparent but readily distinguishable from her surroundings. A copy of this photograph remains in the Save the Bowen archives. The picture is not the only evidence of the presence of the nurse, as many visiting the hospital have confirmed seeing the same apparition standing in the second-story window.

The nurse's ward is at the opposite end of the hallway. The small, dormitory-style rooms were each shared by two nurses. The sound of doors opening and closing and the sound of women giggling and laughing can frequently be heard in this area.

Morris next led us upstairs to the third floor of the Bowen. She explained that this floor had formerly housed the men's living quarters. There is a large, metal gate at the south end of the corridor that was installed in the 1960s to separate part of the hallway from a communal area. This gate frequently can be heard raising and falling of its own volition. Those investigating the sounds later report that the gate is always raised up and nothing appears disturbed.

There are also medical treatment rooms on the third floor, with some of these in use as late as the 1960s. Many controversial "treatments" occurred on this floor, including partial and full lobotomies. The third floor contains the observation room, where these patients were sent to recover. The guide related that a grandmother and granddaughter were taking a tour and stopped in the observation room. Unbeknownst to the grandmother, her granddaughter left her alone in the room and wandered out into the hallway. The grandmother reported feeling an icy hand on

This metal gate on the third-floor main living quarters can be heard opening and closing in the empty hall.

A nurse, whose spirit is said to now haunt the grounds, hung himself from this attic of the Bowen Building in the 1960s.

her shoulder, which then moved to take a firm grasp on her upper arm. She turned to admonish her granddaughter to put her gloves on because her hands were so icy cold but was startled to discover she was alone in the room. Morris recounted that the method nurses used to gain the attention of wayward patients was to initially take them by the shoulder, and if they proved unresponsive, to gently guide them by the arm. Apparently one of the spirits had attempted to guide the grandmother from the room by taking her shoulder, and when that failed, had gently taken her by the arm. The parties were considerably shaken by this encounter and wasted no time in leaving the hospital.

The next stop on the tour was the attic of the Bowen Building. The attic has high, exposed-beamed ceilings and appears in much the same condition as it would have during Dr. Zeller's tenure. This area was mainly used for storage of hospital supplies but was also used by the nurses for a break area. The dormer windows and high ceilings provided excellent cross-ventilation, and the view from the attic is magnificent, encompassing the wide Illinois River as well as the downtown Peoria skyline. The center part of the attic contains the original elevator that would have been in use during Dr. Zeller's time at the hospital. Toward the end of his life, Dr. Zeller lived in the Bowen Building and took a keen interest in every aspect of hospital administration. Part of his oversight involved making frequent forays into the attic to inventory the equipment and furniture at the hospital. There are reports that the figure of Dr. Zeller can still be seen exiting the elevator and walking directly across the attic floor to the window, which commanded an excellent view of his beloved hospital grounds and the patients below.

A less benevolent presence also inhabits the middle attic. Morris related that a former nurse at the site was angered and upset by the changes at the hospital that occurred in the 1960s. One of these developments was the removal of occupational therapy for patients, which left many of these poor souls depressed and directionless. The nurse was so upset by the changes that had occurred, as well as rumors of future downsizing, that he became overwhelmed and suicidal. One night, he took the elevator up to the center of the attic and ascended the metal staircase that led to the storage loft. Once at the top of the stairs, the nurse took a length of rope and hung himself from the rafters. He died at the scene, and his hanging body was not discovered by personnel until two days later.

Morris related that this ghost remains at the site, and the sound of heavy boots thudding on metal can be heard slowly ascending the staircase as the nurse repeatedly returns to the site of his final moments on earth. Visitors and workers also frequently report the sound of heavy, labored breathing in the area, as though the sounds of his last struggle still linger in the air here. This area is also subject to mysterious mists that rise from nowhere and form at the top of the staircase, as well as sudden rushes of icy cold air. Local legend maintains that those passing by the hospital on a moonlit night can look up into the middle windows of the attic and see the silhouette of the hung man still swinging silently from the rafters.

At the far north end of the attic, there is another entity referred to as the "Woman in White." Her real name was Anne Stuart, and she was a housekeeper at the hospital until her death in 1933. There are many stories surrounding her death, including that she died after contracting an illness during her rounds. Another more lurid account maintains that Anne Stuart was in love with a married doctor at the hospital and following his rejection of her affections jumped from the attic window to her death on the ground below. She is a bustling and efficient spirit, moving throughout the areas of the attic and overseeing the administration of long-since-discarded inventory and hospital supplies. She is often heard singing religious tunes as she carries out her duties. Those visiting the hospital frequently ask the source of the songs they hear and are chilled when informed they are hearing a voice from beyond the grave. Anne can also be seen by those outside the Bowen Building, her silhouette reflected as she walks past the attic windows at the north end of the hospital.

The last stop on the tour was the hospital basement and was by far the most haunting and allegedly haunted area of the hospital. Before descending, Morris warned that those visiting the basement often reported feelings of being watched or followed. There are sounds of doors opening and closing of their own volition, as well as strange, dark shapes seen moving up and down the basement corridor.

At the end of the hall at the north end of the basement is the former boiler room, where one of the most active spirits of the Bowen Building remains to carry out his duties. The ghost is a former boiler worker whose job was to add coal to the boiler, which provided heat and power to the building. In Dr. Zeller's time, the coal was brought in by wagon and deposited at the wide doors outside the cellar boiler room. Those working in this area then shoveled the coal inside and kept the fires burning for the hospital. Morris related that this former worker took his job very seriously and would not allow the patients in the boiler room for their own safety. This spirit is one of the most menacing at the hospital and appears to visitors and harshly warns them not to remain in the room. EVPs in this area have picked up the sound of a man's voice, sounding in a warning manner.

Directly next to the boiler room is one of the entrances to the many tunnels that connected most of the buildings of the hospital. After the hospital closed in the 1970s, numerous homeless took over the site and used the tunnels to hide from authorities. During one such episode, two homeless people fled into the tunnels and were lost inside the dark, bricked areas. According to locals, these unfortunates died a slow, agonizing death. Morris reported that few dare to venture into the tunnels, as noises from within this area can frequently be heard. Whether these sounds emanate from restless spirits or wild animals, the tunnels are a sad and rather fearsome place and contribute to the general feeling of hopelessness and sadness that lingers in the basement.

Next to the tunnel at the north end is the former medical examination room. The numerous drains built into the floor and remnants of overhead lighting eloquently tell of the activities of this room, where autopsies and medical examinations were conducted on the patients who died on the grounds. There are also many reports of medical experimentation in this area. However, these rumors greatly discredit Dr. Zeller, and the practical reasons for the medical examination room are gruesome enough without further tales of dark deeds or illicit testing. In this area, there are reports of dark figures or shadows moving toward the doorway at the end of the room, as well as reports of disembodied voices in deep discussion.

At the conclusion of the tour, Morris requested the group rap the top of the basement banister and sternly admonish the spirits to stay at the hospital. She informed us that since the banister was part of the original hospital construction, it had intimate connections with the grounds and the little ritual would keep any restless or curious spirits in place.

Once back outside in the sunshine, our group was able to take in the scope of the grounds and some of the outside areas of the hospital. Next door to the hospital at the south end is a copse of woods dubbed "Depression Woods." It is reported that in the 1930s a number of patients in the depression ward left the hospital grounds and wandered disconsolately into this wooded area. Sometime during the night, a few of these patients hung themselves in the trees in the woods. The legend is that those passing the woods at night can look up into the trees and see the silhouettes of the bodies hanging from the branches.

Across the street from the Bowen Building at the south end is the industrial building that contained the nurses' dining hall. There was also a kitchen, bakery, laundry, and sewing center at this site. This area has fallen into disrepair, and it is no longer safe for tour groups to venture inside the building.

Richard Weiss purchased the Bowen Building and is currently in the process of restoring areas of this historic site. Tours are available, and information can be accessed via the Internet at www.Peoria-Asylum.com. This is a must-see destination for anyone with an interest in the

Here is the vacant medical examination room in the basement of the Bowen Building.

history of mental health treatment, Illinois history, or supernatural activity. The tours are small, and the guides are very well informed. The cemeteries are accessible and close to the Bowen Building. Full access is given to the site, except those areas deemed too dangerous due to current renovations.

Three

CURSES

Scale of Dragon, Tooth of Wolf, / Witches' Mummy, Maw and Gulf / Of the ravin'd salt Sea shark, / Root of Hemlock digg'd i' the dark, / Liver of Blaspheming Jew, / Gall of Goat, and Slips of Yew / Silver'd in the Moon's Eclipse, / Nose of Turk, and Tartar's lips, / Finger of Birth-strangled Babe / Ditch-deliver'd by a Drab, / Make the Gruel thick and slab: / Add thereto a Tiger's Chaudron, / For the Ingredients of our Cauldron. / Double, double toyle and trouble' / Fire burn and Cauldron bubble. / Cool it with a Baboon's blood, / Then the Charm is firm and good.
—William Shakespeare, *Macbeth*, act 4, scene 1

Curses have an ancient history and in the Middle Ages were taken as a serious and present threat. The word *curse* comes from the Old English *curs* and means "a prayer for harm of evil." The scope of a curse can range from something relatively benign, such as hair loss, to something as dramatic as the downfall of an empire. Early physicians commonly diagnosed "curse" when the cause of an illness was unknown. Curses became a mainstream source of expression in Elizabethan England and were highly descriptive and imaginative. The principle purpose of the curse is for revenge, but they can also be used to protect land, homes, or grave sites. Curses placed on families may be dormant for years and once placed can continue for generations.

The Gray Curse
In the 1830s, Andrew and Mary Gray bought and cultivated a plot of land on Monroe Street in downtown Peoria. The Grays were hardworking Irish immigrants. Andrew Gray was a commissioner and forwarder, assisting newly arrived visitors in the shipment and placement of their household goods. The couple lived in a two-story home at 105 North Monroe Street at the site of the present-day Peoria Public Library, Main Street branch.

According to local legend, "Old Lady Gray" was an avid gardener and lovingly cultivated the land around the home. Sometime in the 1830s, Old Lady Gray's brother died in a neighboring state and her teenage nephew came to live with the elderly couple. According to reports of the time, the nephew was a ne'er-do-well and scalawag. He refused to get a job and spent his days drinking and socializing with the crowd that loitered around the stores on the Illinois River bank. He was described as lazy and without morals and was in constant conflict with the village of Peoria authorities due to his drinking and carousing. He was a source of constant disappointment and grief to Old Lady Gray.

At roughly the same time the Gray nephew came to town, a fresh-faced young lawyer moved to Peoria and rented a pine shanty for his law firm. He obtained a piece of wood and painted a sign in black lettering. "David Davis – Attorney at Law." Davis's first client was the drunken and lazy nephew of Old Lady Gray. Davis's reputation grew as he repeatedly defeated the local village attorney in that gentleman's attempts to prosecute the nephew for his exploits. Eventually Davis became concerned about the debt that the Grays were incurring in his representation, and he decided to use the mortgage on the Gray property to secure his attorney fees.

On November 10, 1847, the Grays entered into a trust deed to David Davis for lot 7, block 27, in the original town of Peoria. The mortgage on the property eventually came due, and David

This drawing shows the Gray residence at 105 North Monroe Street, present-day site of Peoria Public Library and the Gray ghost. (Courtesy of the Peoria Public Library, Oakford Collection.)

Davis demanded his attorney fees. The Grays refused to pay the fees, arguing that they had never signed the mortgage paper. David Davis brought a lawsuit against the Grays to foreclose on the mortgage. During the litigation, the Grays vehemently and repeatedly denied ever signing the mortgage, but the physical evidence was against them. David Davis introduced the notarized mortgage document as proof of his claim and won the case. In her anger, Old Lady Gray turned her nephew from her home. Homeless, he wandered the streets of the village drunk and angry, cursing his family. He eventually disappeared. His bloated body was later found in the Illinois River. The Grays were inconsolable. Local legend reports that, in her grief and anger, Old Lady Gray pointed her finger to heaven and called on God to witness the injustice that had been wrought against her family. She cursed the ground of her homestead on Monroe Street with "thorns and thistles, ill luck, sickness and death to its every owner and occupant."

David Davis was now the owner of the cursed land. The soil that had once been fertile and green under Old Lady Gray's careful cultivation now refused to bear anything but spindly weeds. The house was deserted and was soon overrun with vermin and rats. Locals feared both the curse of the house and the rumors of a spirit on the premises. Those passing by at night claimed they could hear the ghost of Old Lady Gray's nephew at the front door, crying and pleading with the old woman for forgiveness and mercy. None of the locals would agree to assist in the maintenance of the house or grounds, and the once well-groomed site became a ramshackle eyesore in the downtown area.

The house and grounds were not the only victims of the curse. David Davis never recaptured his earlier popularity. The Grays had been a couple of notable honesty and integrity in the village, and their misfortunes were pitied by most in the area. Shortly after obtaining his judgment order against the Grays, David Davis moved to Bloomington. He would never take possession of the cursed land.

The old Gray house remained abandoned and overgrown. One winter night, the old homestead inexplicably caught fire. The townspeople hurriedly assembled to extinguish the flames, but the effort was in vain. The house burned to the ground, the flames rising high in a light that could be seen throughout the village. As the fire burned, many of those in attendance claimed they saw the figure of Old Lady Gray in the flames, dancing on the grounds and laughing with delight over its destruction. Shortly after the fire, the ground was sold to pay the property taxes. The land remained overgrown with choking weeds, and people would cross the street in order not to pass too near the cursed ground.

Eventually a new home was built on the site and the rooms let for rent. The site of the old house was rented by ex-governor Thomas Ford and his wife. At this point Old Lady Gray's curse intersected with a second curse, doubly dooming the ex-governor. Ford had entered politics as a circuit judge from Peoria and advanced politically, eventually becoming governor of the state. As governor, he refused to repudiate state bonds issued by the preceding administration for a failed internal improvement system and for the construction of the Illinois and Michigan Canal. Governor Ford paid off the state debt by raising taxes. There was an uprising by a group of Mormon leaders in Carthage, led by Joseph Smith. Governor Ford was accused by each side of partiality, and he finally had to send soldiers to Nauvoo to end the guerilla warfare that had broken out there. Joseph Smith put a curse of death to Governor Ford and the entire Ford household.

Regardless of the accuracy of either curse, the Ford family had more than its share of misfortune. Ex-governor Ford returned to Peoria in 1846. He was in debt and aged beyond his years. He was described thusly by a local editor: "A man, old and feeble, a chip of a hat on, with cotton strings around it, an old jeans coat, no vest, and two Kentucky pantaloons and his legs running through them for about 8 inches, a pair of thick winter socks, brogan shoes with no strings, a clay pipe sticking out of his mouth and puffing like a blacksmith's bellows."

The Fords' three daughters all died of consumption within a brief period. His wife Frances Ford died on October 12, 1850, and Governor Ford died shortly thereafter, a broken and forgotten man. A newspaper account at the time reported that ex-governor Ford died in poverty in rented rooms at the home of Andrew Gray on North Monroe street. The Fords were buried in Springdale cemetery. In 1872, their son Tom Ford was mistaken for a cattle rustler and killed. His brother Sewell sought to avenge his brother's death and killed some of the vigilantes responsible. Sewell himself was killed shortly thereafter.

The site of the Ford home was once again left to decay on the cursed ground. The townspeople believed the site was haunted, and no one wanted to be subject to the curse. The Ford home was eventually demolished. In time, a downstate grocer purchased part of the land and gave it to one of his father's ex-slaves, Tom Lindsay. Lindsay had been freed by the Emancipation Proclamation and built a small shanty at exactly the spot of the old Gray home. Three months after his purchase, Lindsay's house was struck by lightning and burned to the ground. After the fire, Lindsay was informed of the curse on the land by some of the local townspeople. Lindsay had a healthy respect for legends and folklore but needed a place to live and owned the land on Monroe Street. So he built another home at the site. To combat the powers of darkness, Lindsay was given a housewarming gift of a petrified rabbit's foot from a local graveyard. He buried the petrified rabbit's foot under the front door of his new home. To further shield himself from the Gray curse, Lindsay obtained horseshoes for every room in the house and hung them up with sinews from a kingfisher's foot. Lindsay's precautions apparently paid off, for he was able to live at the home for the next 25 years, apparently without incident.

Following Lindsay's death, a local businessman built an ornate home at the site of the former Lindsay house and brought his young bride to live with him there. Tragically, the bride died within the year, and the stories of the curse once again circulated throughout the village of Peoria.

The remaining portion of the Gray lot was eventually purchased by a local banker, who built yet another home at the site. Once again a new bride was brought onto the cursed property, and the happy couple was blessed within a short time by the birth of a boy. However, their happiness was short-lived, for soon after the birth of her child the bride lay dead, and her infant son soon followed her to the grave. The banker eventually recovered from his grief and remarried. His new wife also bore him a son. However, it was soon noted by the inhabitants of the house that the child could not stand warmth or fire. He would cry out if taken near a fireplace, and many visitors were surprised to find him sleeping in the cold front hallway of the home on a raw, winter day. Eventually the boy died, and his mother was taken to Minneapolis to recover her sanity.

The next inhabitant of the cursed site was a boarding housekeeper. Her daughter drowned in Lake Peoria, and her son fell from a hot-air balloon and was killed. For a time, a firm of milliners took over the property to use the site for their business. This venture was short-lived, as they spent much of their time and energy in attempting to locate the source of the strange and foul odor they claimed permeated the air, sickening those present and driving away the clientele.

Curse of the Peoria Public Library

The first library services in Peoria began on October 27, 1855. The Reverend J. R. McFarland and a group of friends gathered together a small collection of books in a room in the 100 block of South Adams Street. A second library was started in November of that year by another small group pooling their books and resources on the same block. In 1855, there were two different libraries providing services in the small village of Peoria: the Peoria Mercantile Library and the Peoria Library. The two libraries were consolidated in 1856 as the Peoria City Library and moved to a building at the site of the Apollo Theater. This remained the city library for 10 years.

Here is the Peoria Public Library reading room in 1915. (Courtesy of the Peoria Public Library, Oakford Collection.)

In 1880, the city of Peoria voted to establish the Peoria Free Public Library that would be supported by local taxes. The Peoria Public Library was established at the corner of Adams and Fulton Streets, where second-floor rooms were rented.

The directors of the Peoria Public Library closed the deal for the purchase of a new site for the library on Thursday, June 28, 1894. The site was at the corner of Monroe Street, opposite the government building at present-day 111–115 North Monroe Street. The original property consisted of three separate lots; lot 7, lot 8, and lot 9. Thirty-six feet on Main Street was purchased from Mrs. Thomas Lindsay and 72 feet from Dr. Loughbridge. The total price was $16,000.

The Peoria Public Library purchased the remainder of the land on Monroe Street in 1894 and erected a handsome, three-story brick library building in 1895. The cornerstone for the new building was dedicated on September 20, 1895.

On November 5, 1891, library board member Erastus S. Willcox was appointed as head librarian. In 1872, Willcox had drawn up legislation that would provide for a free library supported by taxation that was passed by the Illinois state legislature. The new library was open to the public on February 12, 1897, and librarian Willcox gave a moving address to the public on the importance of education and expansion of library services. Willcox was a scholar and educator and was responsible for selecting a number of books that became the prize of the Peoria library book collection. He was a gentleman of the old school and wore a long black alpaca coat at the library even after such apparel had gone out of style. Willcox was vehement in insisting gentlemen entering the library remove their hats and would frequently chastise vagrants or children loitering the halls or in the stairways.

Unfortunately, public service did not appease the curse of the library. While walking to the library in the early afternoon on March 30, 1915, Willcox was struck by a streetcar on the corner of Main Street and Glen Oak Avenue. According to eyewitnesses at the time, he had been attempting to cross Main Street when he was struck by an outbound streetcar. The car had sounded its gong, but Willcox appeared not to hear the alarm. The motorman avoided hitting him directly, but the fender of the car knocked him down. Onlookers reported he had a deep gash in the back of his skull and was taken unconscious to Proctor Hospital where attempts to revive him were unsuccessful. He died a few hours later.

The death of Willcox did not end the curse, and tragedy continued to strike subsequent librarians. Willcox's successor, S. Patterson Prouse, attended a meeting of the library board of directors on December 14, 1921, at 4:00 p.m. Prouse showed no signs of illness during the meeting and engaged in a spirited discussion regarding library bonds. As the meeting adjourned at 4:40 p.m., Prouse stood up to leave the room. He was nearly to the door when he collapsed and lost consciousness. Dr. A. J. Foerter had an office across the street from the library. He was immediately summoned to the scene and administered strong heart stimulants but could not resuscitate the fallen librarian. Dr. Foerter later opined that Prouse was dead when he hit the ground. The curse of the library had apparently claimed another victim.

Following the sudden and untimely death of Prouse, the library association sought a replacement with similar drive and vision who could reorganize the library system and deal with the growing number of volumes. Dr. Edwin Wiley accepted the position of librarian of the Peoria Public Library on May 12, 1922. He was energetic and creative and successfully reorganized the library system. Up to his appointment, the library had been on a "closed shelf" system, whereby the public was required to ask for books that were kept secured in storage stacks. Dr. Wiley implemented the "open shelf" system, where the books were kept on open shelves accessible to the general public.

Dr. Wiley was also interested in community service and during his tenure became a prominent figure in Peoria social circles. He implemented the Bedside Book Service, where books would be brought to the invalid and infirm at area hospitals. His success would prove short-lived. Dr. Wiley died unexpectedly from poisoning at his home at 414 Fredonia Avenue on October 20, 1924. His

The Peoria Public Library Main Street branch is the house of the Gray curse today.

wife reported to officials that she awoke at daybreak on October 20 and heard her husband groaning in bed. Dr. Wiley told his wife that he had taken arsenic from the collection of chemicals his son, a student at Bradley Polytechnic Institute, kept in the basement of their home. Mrs. Wiley called their treating physician, who arrived at the home and discovered Dr. Wiley in bed, hovering on the edge of consciousness. The doctor made an attempt to get Dr. Wiley to emit the poison, but this was unsuccessful. Dr. Wiley was rushed to the hospital and had his stomach pumped. Dr. Wiley was conscious and able to speak but gave no explanation as to why he had taken the arsenic. Dr. Wiley died later that day from arsenic poisoning. It was later reported that Dr. Wiley had a history of depressive disorder, and a year prior to his suicide, he had swallowed veronal and become seriously ill. He remained in a sanitarium for months but eventually recovered and was able to resume his duties until his death. The local citizenry attributed Dr. Wiley's strange death to the old Gray curse.

Although there are reports of inaccuracies and errors in the story of the curse, especially with respect to the Gray family, the legend of the Gray curse continues. The many unexpected and tragic deaths and accidents associated with the site remain unexplained to this day.

Even if the curse is the stuff of fiction and folklore, there have been a number of strange occurrences at the library. A school superintendent, Newton Dougherty, blew up a safe in the library in 1907 to cover up his embezzlement of school funds. At the time, the school district's offices were in the library. In another bizarre twist, the library became part of a blackmail plot following the death of George P. McNear Jr. The widow of McNear received two letters instructing her that the name of the murderer would be revealed if she placed $1,000 in a special drawer on the third-floor education room of the Peoria Public Library. She contacted the authorities and was instructed to place paper strips in an envelope and place it in the drawer. On March 23, 1947, a father and son, William Anthony Gibson and William John "Billy" Gibson, entered the library, went to the third floor, and retrieved the envelope. They were quickly arrested by the local authorities who were waiting at the scene. In their defense, their attorney argued that the men did have the information they offered, like the name of McNear's murderer; however, no proof or testimony was offered at trial as to this evidence. The father and son also alleged their appearance at the library was purely coincidental. Despite their protestations of innocence, the pair was convicted and ordered to serve a lengthy prison sentence.

The Curse and Aftermath

The present Peoria Public Library Main Street branch opened on March 23, 1968. There are rumors the curse of the Peoria Public Library remains intact despite the passing years and renovations. The repeated tragedies that have struck the former librarians and their untimely deaths have been attributed to the Gray curse.

The Main Street branch of the public library reportedly continues to play host to a number of spirits. There are stories the building is haunted by the ghost of Erastus Willcox. Visitors have reported seeing a man dressed in early-1900s garb turning the corners of the stacks or walking through the halls. A common explanation given for hauntings is work left unfinished by the deceased. Does Willcox still try to resolve the library problems and assist in public education?

Many visiting the basement of the library have been taken by surprise by strange gusts of cold air that seem to have no origin. There have also been reports of the sound of stacks of books toppling to the floor, but upon investigation nothing in the area appears disturbed. Doors are said to open and close of their own volition. Many have reported hearing the sound of voices murmuring in conversation in the empty basement rooms. There have also been reports of ghostly faces appearing in glass reflections or mirrors.

Despite these tales, the library remains a friendly and inviting spot, just as it must have been for its first patrons at the dawn of the 20th century. Despite the "curse," most agree that there remain few pleasanter places in Peoria to spend an evening than lost in the stacks at the Peoria Public Library.

Four

RESTLESS BONES

All the stories of ghosts and goblins that he had heard in the afternoon
now came crowding upon his recollection. The night grew darker and darker; the
stars seemed to sink deeper in the sky, and driving clouds occasionally hid them
from his sight. He had never felt so lonely and dismal. He was moreover, approaching
the very place where many of the scenes of the ghost stories had been laid.
—Washington Irving, *The Legend of Sleepy Hollow*

Peoria: City of the Dead

In August 1673, the first Christian burial took place in the village of Peoria. Louis Joliet and Pere Jacques Marquette made contact with the Peoria tribe in 1673 on the way down the Illinois River from the Straits of Michilimackinac in Canada. On their return upriver in August 1673, they stopped to visit the tribe and in passing converted as many as possible to Christianity. A dying child was brought to receive baptism and shortly thereafter died and was buried on the edge of the Illinois River. It would be nearly 200 years before a formal cemetery for the village of Peoria was established.

In the early days of cemetery burial, cemeteries were established in proximity to the centers of commerce and religious institutions. This practice allowed bodies to remain for as short an amount of time as possible above ground and provided a reminder to the living of the ephemeral nature of human existence.

Like many of the towns established in the early 1800s, Peoria is built on grounds of many of its former cemeteries. Excavation of buildings for the advancement of the new village of Peoria (established in 1797) frequently resulted in excavation of the graves of either Native Americans or French settlers. These graves were excavated in every section of present-day downtown, with bodies frequently recovered on Liberty and Water Streets. Many of the buildings in the downtown area and along Adams Street allegedly have skeletons that remain buried in the basements under layers of lime. There was a French burial ground that was used in the old village of Peoria until about 1839 that ran along Adams Street to the north. This cemetery is believed to have been located to the northeast of present-day downtown, which would have been the outfields of the new village of Peoria (site of the old village of Peoria). The *Peoria Star* reported on June 22, 1899, that the ancient remains of a human skeleton had been uncovered at the head of Mary Street in the area that would have been encompassed by the old village of Peoria. One of the more grisly discoveries revealed a man who was lying on his side, presumptively having turned over at some point after burial. Another coffin that was discovered on Liberty Street contained a skeleton with a number of elaborate circular metallic plates around the head, and the wrists of the skeleton were adorned with metal bands, stamped with the word *Montreal*. The body also had a large ornate crucifix around the neck and a silver teaspoon was found in the grave.

It is probable the French originally living at this site had established a Catholic cemetery at the site, but no evidence remains other than the continued excavation of bodies. The remains of at least 15 other persons had been recovered in the area between Adams Street and the Illinois

River, which raised the possibility of a cemetery at the old village of Peoria that existed between 1673 and 1723. It was reported that the area from Adams Street to the alley was full of human bones. These graves were either those of the original Frenchmen in the area at the time or Native Americans who had embraced Christianity and been rewarded with a Christian burial.

The village of Peoria changed location in the late 1700s, and a group of pioneers settled in what was then known as La Ville de Maillet, or the new village of Peoria. This was also the site of the former Fort Clark. The new village of Peoria was located at Liberty and Fulton Streets, extending from Washington Street to the west and Adams Street to the east. As Peoria continued to expand, new bodies were uncovered and the remains were moved to the outskirts of present-day downtown, likely to the site of the old French cemetery on Adams Street. This French cemetery was described by Charles Ballance as located at block 35, which would be the area bounded by South Adams Street on the west, Harrison Street on the north, South Washington Street on the east, and Franklin Street on the south. There was also a Catholic cemetery directly across the river from the new village of Peoria on the Tazewell side, at the site of the present-day waterfront park. This was a small, family cemetery of the Moushon family (or Mougeon in French).

In 1839, Peoria opened its first public city cemetery. The city cemetery was located at the present-day Lincoln Street branch of the Peoria Public Library at 1312 West Lincoln Avenue. Although this cemetery was later moved, many of the bodies remained at the site. In the 1830s, there was also a Native American village and cemetery located at the site of the present-day Exposition Gardens. By 1849, there were only two established cemeteries in Peoria, the aforementioned city cemetery and the Masonic cemetery, which opened in 1844 at Perry Avenue and Jackson Street. These early cemeteries could not keep up with the pace of rapid city development. As expansion continued, multiple building excavations in downtown Peoria resulted in the discovery of skeletons and skulls. The majority of these remains were transferred to Springdale Cemetery; however, many remained at the site. There was such a prevalence of bones and skulls in the downtown area that local aldermen entered a formal complaint that schoolboys were using the skulls of former voters in the district as footballs.

In 1852, St. Mary's parish established a cemetery in the northern part of the city between Galena Road and the Illinois River, bounded by Rock Island Railroad on the east and North Adams Street on the west. This cemetery did not prosper and was abandoned by 1857 and overgrown with weeds.

By 1857, the population of the new village of Peoria had jumped to 17,482, pushing the limits of the established cemeteries. The following excerpt was taken from *Peoria Weekly* on November 12, 1869:

> Workmen laying tracks for the first horsecar street railway dug up three skeletons at Adams and Liberty Streets—two of them wearing army uniforms and one believed to be a Native American. The supposed soldiers had been wrapped in cloaks that bore buttons with the insignia USA. No garments were found near the other burial. Peter Menard, an old-timer from Tazewell County, recalled that a soldier stationed at Fort Clark (Peoria) shortly after the War of 1812 was shot and killed by a Native American named Big Foot and that he was buried about where the bones were uncovered.

The newspaper account reported that some of the spectators tried to get the bones for private admiration, but a couple of gentlemen gathered them up in a box and announced their intention of giving them a decent burial in Springdale Cemetery.

In 1873, the Peoria Hebrew cemetery was established on seven acres in Haskell's subdivision in Peoria County. In 1874, Moffat Cemetery was established in the 3900 block of South Adams

Street on land purchased from the United States government. The cemetery was closed by public health officials in 1902. In 1882, Bishop John Lancaster Spaulding opened a new cemetery and transferred the bodies from Old St. Mary's to the new site located at what is now Sterling Avenue in the west bluff. The site of the old cemetery was used for manufacturing.

As Peoria became more populated, the value of land in the heavily populated areas increased and was used for the needs of the living rather than the dead. There was also a growing awareness of sanitation and the possibility of contamination of nearby drinking water if bodies were buried too close to the general population. Eventually it became popular for burials to take place in the country, rather than near the center of town.

As late as 1962, graves continued to be discovered near the downtown area. In that year, a grave and skeleton were discovered in the backyard of a residence at 1029 South Brown Street, four blocks from the foot of South Street.

In 2008, the city approved plans to add a 15,000-square-foot expansion to the Lincoln Branch Library. The library was built at the site of the Public Graveyard, later renamed the City Cemetery. The City Cemetery was in operation from approximately 1841 to 1875, and during that time, as many as 700 individuals were reportedly interred at the site. The City Cemetery closed in 1875, and the remains of at least 320 of the dead were removed to Springdale Cemetery. Many of the family members of those buried at the site protested the removal of the remains and obtained injunctions to halt further excavation of City Cemetery. This legal maneuver halted the transfer of remains in the late 1880s, and the land was protected from development in perpetuity. However, the land was still subject to local improvements. It was reported that in 1903, ditch diggers discovered remains from 8–10 graves at the site. The Lincoln Branch Library was built at site in 1911. At the time of initial construction, it was reported that at least five graves had been discovered. The final disposition of these remains is unknown.

In 2008, the library obtained a permit to excavate the property bordering the Lincoln Branch Library and remove any remains found there. Initial excavations in June 2009 resulted in the discovery of 66 burial shafts and a mass grave containing 48 infant coffins tightly packed together. Under the Human Skeletal Remains Protection Act, human remains must be removed, identified if possible, and reinterred elsewhere. Although there are no records that document the number of bodies buried in the old City Cemetery, it is estimated that over 120 graves could remain.

The Lincoln Branch Library has long been the subject of many tales of supernatural activity and alleged hauntings. It is reported that a young mother and her infant child were buried together at the site, and the phantom woman wanders the grounds, holding her child in her arms and weeping inconsolably. There are also reports the site is haunted by the ghost of a Civil War soldier, still dressed in battle uniform, who appears in the mist and just as quickly disappears. Regardless of the veracity of these tales, the Lincoln Branch Library and grounds remain a poignant reminder of Peoria's early history.

Peoria was built on the bones of its ancestors, and its cemeteries are an integral and vital part of the city's colorful history and charm. They also provide a potential explanation for the many reports of ghosts and spirits that allegedly roam the downtown area.

Establishment of Springdale Cemetery

In 1851, a site within the heart of the city was chosen for a public cemetery. The site selected was on a bluff, overlooking the Illinois River and Lower Peoria Lake, approximately two miles from Peoria's central business district. Local money was raised to pay for purchasing and enclosing the grounds to create the cemetery. The cemetery was organized in 1854 by the Springdale Cemetery Association and chartered in February 1855. The Springdale Cemetery was incorporated in 1855 by Thomas Baldwin, Hervey Lightner, William A. Hall, and Onslow Peters. It is the second-oldest cemetery in the state of Illinois.

Springdale Cemetery's gatekeeper cottage on the Perry Street entrance is currently undergoing restoration.

Prior to the establishment of Springdale Cemetery, there were six or seven small cemeteries in the very center of town. The old city cemetery was on the present site of the Lincoln Library; the upper and lower burial grounds were along the Illinois River near Franklin and Adams Streets; the Masonic cemetery was at Glendale, Jackson, and Bryan Streets; the Jewish cemetery was on South Adams Street; the Moffat's Cemetery was on the south side; and old St. Mary's Cemetery was in Averyville.

When the Springdale Cemetery was built, the main road on the south ran toward the city, and a shady dirt road led to the entrance. A streetcar trolley ran up Perry Street in Peoria to the cemetery. At its inception, the cemetery encompassed 200 acres and was surrounded by a board fence. The lower entrance to the cemetery (closed in 1958) at the end of Perry Avenue (formerly Springdale Road) was adjacent to Birket's Hollow, which in 1862 was a Union training camp and later would become Glen Oak Park. The Fort Clark Horse Railway ran mule cars to the entrance of Springdale Cemetery. In 1874, streetcars were used to pull coffins and funeral parties out to the end of the tracks, because the dirt roads would turn to mud, preventing carriages from getting through. By 1880, there were 6,000 to 7,000 bodies buried in the cemetery. Prices of the lots during that time ranged from 30¢ to 50¢ per square foot.

The cemetery grounds originally included a holding vault built into a bluff below Soldier's Hill. Bodies could be stored in the vault for 20 days in order to allow the families' time to make funeral arrangements. If the family was using Springdale as the final resting place, the only charge for this service was a $1 fee when the vault was opened and the body was taken to the grave site. If, however, the family wished to take the body to a different cemetery, there was a storage and removal charge of $10 for adults and $5 for children. In the cold winter months, bodies could be kept in the vault until the burial could be completed in the spring thaw. Today gas flames under steel covers thaw the ground and a backhoe is used to dig the graves. Although the vault has since been removed, the depression in the bluff can still be seen today.

There were two entrances to the cemetery, one on Prospect Hill Road and one on the northwest. The Springdale Gatehouse, a craftsman bungalow, was built in 1900 and is located at the lower entrance to the cemetery. The house was originally an office and residence, with a storage vault on the first floor. The house had fallen into disrepair, although it has recently become the subject of renovation efforts. Also at the lower entrance were stone fence piers, a wrought-iron gate and fence, and an ironworks. Just outside the original lower entrance was a single-acre pet cemetery that has subsequently been moved to an area next to the gazebo. Of note in the cemetery is the Lightner monument in the valley across from "the Cove." Over 40 feet tall and constructed of Colorado granite, the monument was erected in 1874 to mark the plot of Hervey Lightner and towers over the valley. The upper entrance to Springdale is located on Prospect Road (formerly Pacific Avenue). A brick gatehouse once stood at this site but has since been removed. Another entrance to the cemetery on the north side of War Memorial Drive is only opened when special access is required.

Even early on there were many problems with maintenance of the grounds, as residents would bury family members and then move from the area, leaving behind a cemetery quickly choking with weeds and debris. To preserve the cemetery, legislation was passed to incorporate the Springdale Cemetery Association, and the charter provided that funds should be used for maintenance of the land and graves.

A visitor to the cemetery today has the pleasure of surveying a graceful and shaded site where over 78,000 graves are set within a parklike setting of 230 acres of oak savanna hills and valleys. That same lucky visitor might also have an encounter with the famed Lady in White.

Here is the ditch across from the Lightner monument, where Gerald T. Thompson left the body of Mildred Hallmark.

The Lady in White

It was a balmy and rainy night in Peoria on June 16, 1935. The rain pounded on the tops of the streetcars passing in front of Bishop's Cafeteria downtown. The Sunday evening slowly passed by, with the small town engaged in its recreations and pleasures: watching movies, eating out, attending church events, and socializing with friends and family. No one could have predicted this quiet night would produce one of the most sensational and shocking murders in Peoria's history.

Nineteen-year-old Mildred Hallmark was a pretty auburn-haired girl and recent graduate from the Catholic school, Academy of Our Lady. Mildred was born on April 19, 1916, the daughter of John and Esther Hallmark. The family moved to Peoria in 1928. Mildred was working as a waitress at Bishop's Cafeteria on June 16, 1935. Bishop's Cafeteria was located at the site of the current planned Peoria Riverfront Museum. The area was once the hub of town, with bars, theaters, and restaurants running the length of Main Street and beyond.

Mildred left Bishop's Cafeteria after her shift at 8:30 p.m. with a fellow employee, John McGinnis. John would later testify that they had not been out together before that night. He was a Bradley student and worked as a busboy at Bishop's. The couple arranged to see *The People's Enemy* at the Rialto at 9:00 p.m. John testified that Mildred tried to telephone home to inform her parents of her plans but could not get an answer.

It was a wet night, and the pair dashed up rain-soaked Jefferson Street to see the movie. After the film ended, Mildred again tried to call her parents' to inform them of her whereabouts but could not reach them. The couple left the theater at 11:00 p.m. and tried to catch a country club streetcar at the corner of Main and Jefferson Streets. They missed this car and boarded a Knoxville Avenue streetcar at the corner of Main and Perry Streets at 11:15 p.m. The couple got out at Knoxville and Pennsylvania Avenues to catch the Peoria Heights streetcar. John McGinnis caught a streetcar back downtown, leaving Mildred waiting for the Heights car. That was the last time John McGinnis saw Mildred Hallmark.

Somewhere between 11:30 p.m. and 2:00 a.m., Mildred Hallmark was brutally raped and murdered. Her nude body was thrown into a ditch at Springdale Cemetery. Her white lace dress was ripped to shreds and wadded up under her arms. Her small white sandals were lying in the dirty sand of the creek bed. Also found was a soggy paper package, containing white yarn, knitting needles, and a partially finished white sweater. Her purse and a diamond ring on her right hand remained with the body, making it clear her death was not the result of a botched robbery.

Mildred's body was found at 8:30 a.m. the following morning in a ditch along Valley Road in Springdale Cemetery, less than two blocks from the Prospect entrance and only four blocks from Mildred's home at 1100 East Maywood Avenue. Her body had been pushed into a ditch along a small retaining wall.

The Lady in White: The Manhunt

With the discovery of Mildred Hallmark's body, "Peoria's Greatest Manhunt" began. The small town was shocked and outraged by the brutal rape and slaying of one of its most innocent residents. Panic swept the area, and women were cautioned to travel in groups and not accept rides from strangers. Many avoided riding the streetcars alone at night.

The people demanded a villain, and scapegoats were pinpointed and brought in by police to assuage the cry for justice. Initial reports indicated there were roustabouts from a local carnival at Prospect Avenue, and an escaped fugitive from Detroit had been spotted in the area about 2:30 a.m. There was also an increase in reports of activities of other "abnormals" or "morons" in the area. A reward of $250 was offered to anyone who could help bring the killer to justice. Police were given orders to arrest anyone picking up a young woman waiting for a streetcar or

PEORIA'S HAUNTED MEMORIES

bus or urging them to accept a ride. Illinois governor Henry Horner contributed $100 to the reward fund.

As the hysteria mounted, many young women came forward with stories of rape and assault committed by a single man. These stories and other tips quickly led to the arrest of 25-year-old Gerald T. (Jerry) Thompson. Gerald was young, athletic, and good-looking. He could sing and play the guitar and had many friends in the area.

Thompson was arrested on June 21, 1935, at the Caterpillar plant in East Peoria at 12:50 p.m. Thompson worked at Caterpillar, Inc., the local tractor maker, with the victim's father, John Hallmark. His workbench was 20 feet from that of John Hallmark, and Thompson had signed a CAT petition to avenge the death of Mildred Hallmark. Thompson had also contributed 25¢ to a flower fund for the funeral.

Due to fears of lynch mob justice, Thompson was moved to the McLean County Jail in Bloomington. On June 23, 1935, Thompson confessed to the murder of Mildred Hallmark. Thompson told police that he had committed a large number of assaults and that Springdale Cemetery was his favorite place to rape these women. He reported that he normally picked up married women, as they put up more of a fight and were more exciting to him sexually. Thompson recorded these escapades in a small black book. Thompson used blackmail to escape prosecution. After he was done raping the women, he would force them to stand nude in front of the headlights of his car and take photographs of them. If they threatened to go to the authorities, Thompson would threaten to expose their adultery to their husbands. This blackmail was surprisingly effective, and Thompson was able to rape scores of women without any police interference. The police also uncovered sex toys and lewd photographs at his home.

Earlier that year, Thompson had confessed some of his sexual escapades to a friend, Sam Sprinkle. Sprinkle had formerly worked with Thompson at Bemis Bag Company in Morton and had known him for four years. Sprinkle would later testify during the trial that Thompson told him he was going to try to pick up at least 52 women in 1934, in order to have one per week. Late in November 1934, Thompson claimed he had already had 54. Thompson showed Sprinkle lewd photographs of himself and nude women on three different occasions and had a number of pornographic books. Sprinkle would later testify he thought Thompson was insane.

In his defense, Thompson claimed that he was not given any food following his arrest until his confession. He also claimed the police offered him leniency and threatened him with possible lynching. Under questioning with a lie detector device from a Northwestern University crime detection laboratory, Thompson made a full confession. During the course of his confession, Thompson reported he had not been beaten or abused and the confession was made of his own free will.

The Lady in White: The Confession
Gerald T. Thompson related that at the time of the murder, he was living with his elderly grandparents at 805 Maryland Avenue in Peoria. On the evening of June 16, 1935, he picked up his girlfriend, Lola Hughes, and took her to the theater. After dropping Hughes off at her home on Machin Street, Thompson cruised the streets of Peoria, looking for a new conquest to add to his growing little black book. At 11:20 p.m., he turned his car onto Knoxville Avenue and followed the streetcar tracks on Knoxville to Pennsylvania Avenue. At the corner of Pennsylvania and Knoxville, Thompson saw Mildred Hallmark standing in her white dress, patiently waiting for the next streetcar. Thompson decided to try to pick up Mildred. He slowed down his 1934 Willys Sedan and leaned over to the open passenger-side window. Thompson had earlier taken the precaution of removing the door handle from the passenger's side of the vehicle, so once his victim was inside she would have no choice but to stay inside. Thompson leaned over and smiled. Thompson was 25 years old, attractive, athletic, and clean-cut. Mildred

would have no reason to expect she would be in any kind of danger and probably would not have been unduly alarmed by the offer of a ride. Thompson asked Mildred how far she was going, and she responded that she had quite a long way to go. Thompson again asked her how far she was going, and Mildred told him to she had to go out to Maywood Avenue, a few miles away. Thompson continued to press Mildred to accept a ride in his car. Mildred knew it was getting late, and if she was not home soon her parents would worry. She looked again for the streetcar and, not seeing its approach, agreed to Thompson's offer of a ride. Thompson opened the passenger-side door for Mildred, and the couple proceeded down Knoxville Avenue.

As Thompson proceeded toward Maywood Avenue, he kept up an easy banter with Mildred, asking her about her work and school. Thompson was accustomed to putting young women at ease and soon had Mildred relaxed and chatting. This state was only temporary. Mildred became concerned when Thompson turned north on Prospect Avenue rather than going south to the her home on Maywood. Thompson continued to drive and ask Mildred questions, but she was increasingly wary. She requested that Thompson take her home, and he acted as though he meant to comply. He turned around at Lake Avenue and headed back south on Prospect toward Maywood. Mildred became even more concerned when, instead of proceeding to Maywood, Thompson turned into the entrance of Springdale Cemetery.

At this point, Mildred still could not believe she was in any real danger. She was only four blocks away from her home and was innocent enough to believe that Thompson would still take her home. She told Thompson that she could not stay out any longer and that she needed to go home. Thompson agreed that she should be at home in bed, but instead of turning the car around he drove down Valley Road into the heart of the cemetery. The only light came from the car headlights as he proceeded down the dark, winding road. By this time, Mildred must have realized she was in trouble. There were no houses close by, and no one in the cemetery at midnight on a Sunday night. Thompson stopped at the bridge at the area of the pond, while Mildred pleaded with him to take her home. He decided to proceed a bit farther before he finished what he had started. He crossed the bridge and stopped by the pond. He ordered Mildred to get in the backseat of the car. A struggle ensued, and Mildred fought and argued with Thompson, still demanding that he take her home. Thompson threatened to hit her. Thompson opened his car door and held the door open for Mildred. She crawled across the front seat and got out of the driver's side door. Thompson was still attempting to convince Mildred to consent to sex with him, but she was adamant that she would not submit. Eventually he grabbed her and twisted her arm around her back. Mildred started to scream. Thompson wrapped his hands around Mildred's throat to stop the screams, and she bit him on his left thumb and scratched the back of his head. Thompson drew back his fist and struck her in the jaw. Mildred lost consciousness and fell across the backseat. Thompson proceeded to tear off her clothes and rape her as she lay unconscious. After he was done, Thompson got out of the car and wiped himself with a rag. He then leaned against the car and had a cigarette. When he was finished, Thompson climbed into the backseat and tried to rouse Mildred. When he could not find a heartbeat, he decided to get rid of Mildred's body.

Although Thompson would later testify he had no intention of harming Mildred, he related that after he raped her he decided to strip her body so she could not be identified by her clothing. He took a pair of scissors from the glove compartment and proceeded to cut her dress to shreds. He also took off her white shoes and stockings and laid them next to her in the backseat. He then got out of the car and got back in the front seat. He decided he would take her to the bridge and dump her body into the Illinois River. He started to drive out of the cemetery toward Prospect Avenue, but before he got to the main road he changed his mind and turned around near the main entrance. He drove back down the hill toward the Lightner monument and got back out of the car. He went to the backseat and dragged

Mildred's body out by the arms. He dumped her over the shallow embankment into the ditch below, leaving her body grotesquely straddling a fallen log. Thompson would later relate in chilling detail that he had no idea if Mildred was dead when he dumped her body and had not bothered to look. He took the coat and clothing he had cut from her and threw it over the bank toward the body. He also took the shoes and stockings and threw those over the bank. Thompson then got back into his car and drove back toward the pond before arriving at a fork in the road. He turned around at the fork and drove his car out of the cemetery, turning left on Prospect Avenue. Thompson returned to his home and went to bed. His grandparents would later relate that Thompson had resumed his usual activities during the day on Monday, working on his car and then working the third shift at Caterpillar. When he arrived at work, he feigned surprise in hearing about the rape-murder and even went so far as to sign a petition, vowing to avenge Mildred's death.

After his confession, Thompson was secretly smuggled to a jail cell in Decatur to await his trial. He would not have long to wait.

The Lady in White: The Trial

The murder trial of Gerald T. Thompson was set for July 22, 1935, at 10:00 a.m. before the Honorable Judge Joseph Daily and a jury of Thompson's peers. The case was held in the third-floor courtroom of the downtown courthouse on Hamilton Street. It was the event of the century. At 7:00 a.m., a crowd began to form at the courthouse doors. In addition to the courtroom seats, benches were provided for maximum capacity. Even this was not enough, and many spectators brought along blankets, which they spread in the rotunda below the courtroom to receive word of the trial and to catch a glimpse of the accused murderer.

The press descended on Peoria en masse, with reporters from Chicago newspapers and *Life* magazine. In order to ensure prompt dissemination of news from the trial, telegraph circuits were installed in the chambers of Judge John Culbertson Jr. A workroom was also set up for reporters, and there were six direct telegraph lines, four telephones, and one radio microphone. Messengers were hired to take copy from the press benches to the wire room.

The courtroom was sticky and oppressive in the mid-July heat, and one enterprising merchant had fans distributed that were printed with advertisements. The audience sought some relief from the short bursts of air, but the press of bodies packed to the maximum limit was almost overwhelming, and many in the audience had to be escorted from the courtroom. A few electric fans were set up to help combat the stifling July temperatures. There were 125 people packed into the courtroom, and the majority of them were women. Many of them realized the trial would interrupt their daily chores, and washday in Peoria was rescheduled. Most brought picnic lunches so they would not lose their seats, and there were many greetings and social exchanges before the trial and during jury breaks. However, the atmosphere remained hushed and solemn. It was the first time many in the audience had been in the same room with an accused murderer.

Prior to the first day of testimony, Thompson was smuggled into town from Decatur and put in the Peoria Jail. The threat of mob justice was still very prevalent, as public sentiment had not cooled in the roasting July heat. But justice had also worked quickly, with the trial set a mere month after the murder. Thompson's cell window overlooked Bishop's Cafeteria, where the victim had worked.

Thompson's mother, Florence Whiteside, had been a patient at Proctor Hospital for two weeks prior to the trial, suffering a nervous collapse. The defense sought a continuance, arguing that the mother's testimony was critical to establish that when Thompson was 15 years old, he formed habits and conducted himself in a manner that proved he was "morally insane." The judge rejected this argument, and the case continued to jury selection.

Springfield Cemetery's gazebo area is the site of the infamous duck pond where Mildred Hallmark was murdered.

Throughout voir dire, the prosecution sought married jurors and men with families as those most inclined to be sympathetic to the deceased and her family. At that time, women were not allowed to serve on jury panels. Jury selection was completed at 3:00 p.m. on July 25, 1935. Fifty-five jurors had been examined; and 43 had been excused. The prosecution had used 11 of its allotted 20 peremptory challenges and excused 6 for cause. The defense used 7 peremptory challenges and had 19 witnesses excused for cause.

During most of the jury selection, Thompson sat with his chin in one hand, fingering his lips or neck, with the other hand draped over the back of the chair. He did not appear unduly concerned but would occasionally whisper to his attorney.

The case against Thompson began with Deputy Coroner Gumm testifying that Mildred's body was lying on its right side with the legs crossed and the thighs higher than the head in the ditch at Springdale Cemetery. The head lay 10 inches from the concrete abutment. A torn dress, slip, and brassiere were rolled under the arms. There were bruises on the chin, discolorations on the neck, and bruises on the knees and scalp. The body was identified with a white purse holding Mildred's library card to the Peoria Public Library.

The victim's sister, Ruby Hallmark, then testified for the state. She testified that Mildred had auburn hair; was five feet, six inches; and weighed 125 pounds. Ruby testified that Mildred had risen early on Sunday, June 16, to go to mass before starting her shift at Bishop's Cafeteria. When she last saw her sister, she was wearing a dark silk dress with small white polka dots with a white collar, cuffs, and a white felt hat. Following Ruby's testimony, the court admitted into evidence a blood-stained, cream-colored brown and white polka dot lace dress, polka dot belt, small brasserie, tea rose pink slip, pair of bloomers, beige silk stockings, white sandals, and a piece of knitting in white wool with knitting needles. The effect on the audience was electrifying. Many who had dozed during the more mundane points of identification testimony craned their heads to get a glimpse of the sad pieces of clothing that told the story of Mildred's final hours. Police also had a pair of Thompson's bloodstained trousers and a bloodstained car cushion from his automobile. The coroner testified that death was due to spinal cord injury when neck was broken.

A witness for the state, John Manias, lived at Manias Manor apartments at the corner of Knoxville and Pennsylvania Avenues. He testified he woke up at between 11:00 and 11:45 to open the window and saw a woman standing by a car. He looked again and testified a man was leading the woman by the arm toward the automobile. He testified there was no struggle. He had known Thompson for five years but could not identify him as the man on the scene. Manias testified that everything he saw in the street occurred in three quarters of a minute.

Detective Charles Welty identified a pair of scissors removed from Thompson's car that had been used to cut the clothes off the body so it could not be identified. The state rested.

In his defense, Thompson's court-appointed attorney, Ren Thurman, gave a 10-minute opening statement, indicating he would show the defendant was sexually insane. Thurman opined that Thompson's father was unnatural sexually, and Thompson inherited this insanity of character. The father had left the family while they were waiting for him after a movie. Thurman also pointed out that Thompson's brother had recently been confined for indecent liberties with a little boy. References were made to "tainted ancestry" and "tainted offspring."

The case was continued until the next morning. There was a frenzy to hear the defense, and a stampede of women pulled the hinges off the courthouse doors at the main entrance and Main Street sides. Several people were knocked down and trampled, but no serious injuries were reported.

The defense called its first witness, Dr. Peter James. Dr. James was the physician for Thompson's mother, Florence Whiteside, who was integral to the defense strategy of sexual insanity. However, Whiteside had a nervous breakdown upon Thompson's arrest, and Dr. James testified it would endanger her life to be present in court. She remained in Proctor Hospital for the duration of the trial. *Curious*

The defense next called Jessie Hughes, the mother of Thompson's sweetheart, Lola Hughes. Jessie Hughes kept a folded newspaper in front of her face while testifying. She testified she had known Thompson for five years and he was always a well-behaved gentleman. She testified the defendant did not smoke, use liquor, or use profanity in her presence.

There were no other witnesses that presented a defense other than that the claimant was well mannered and did not drink alcohol. The jury deliberated a short time and quickly found the defendant guilty of first-degree murder, rejecting the defense argument of manslaughter.

The Lady in White: Swift Justice

Gerald T. Thompson was sent to the Joliet penitentiary on August 17, 1935, and awaited execution set for October 15, 1935. There was an appeal for a new trial, which was denied. Thompson's lawyer sought a writ of supersedeas or executive clemency. There was no response. The case reached the Illinois Supreme Court on October 3, 1935, and the death verdict was upheld.

The argument that this had not been a premeditated crime had now been universally rejected by jury, trial judge, appeals court, supreme court, Gov. Henry Horner, and finally, the appeals board.

Thompson's execution was scheduled for October 15, 1935. His last meal was fried chicken, stuffed olives, wilted head lettuce, and black walnut ice cream. At 10:00 p.m., Thompson, or prisoner No. 1768, was moved into a room upstairs in the prison with the electric chair 40 feet away. The prison barber shaved a small spot on the top of his head to fit a moistened sponge to increase the shock of the electricity. The Reverend Maurice Sammon, pastor of St. Bernard's, walked Thompson to the chair. Two hundred spectators gathered behind a glass partition that separated them from the execution room. It was so crowded that those in front were ordered to get on their knees so the people at the back could see. The victim's father, John Hallmark, was forced to stand on a chair to watch. When asked if he had any last words, Thompson said, "Jesus, forgive my sins. Hope God will accept me. Good-bye."

At 12:15 a.m. Warden Ragen raised his hand and two red bulbs on the wall behind the chair lit up. The body lurched forward against the leather straps. There was a bolt of low voltage and another surge forward with the body straining against the straps. Then two white bulbs came on, and there were two more power surges, the body straightening with each jolt. After the fourth jolt, the prison physician sought a heartbeat. There was none. Thompson had died in two minutes. The undertaker took the body away in a basket.

The tragedy of the Lady in White was finally over, but the legacy of Mildred Hallmark would continue.

Legacy of the Lady in White

Since the death of Mildred Hallmark there have been reports of strange sightings in the Springdale Cemetery. Unexplained lights appear in the cemetery at night, and there are stories of white or yellow globes of light that appear to be attracted to a single headstone or grave. These tales recur particularly in the vicinity of the Lightner monument, which is near the spot where the body of Mildred Hallmark was discovered. The lights are said to rise up from the ground and hover in the area, only to disappear completely moments later. There is no explanation as to the source of these lights.

One source reported that in late 2006 he and a friend were in the cemetery at dusk, down by the gazebo near the site of the former duck pond. As they walked across the bridge, they saw the figure of a young woman wearing a 1930s-style white dress standing near a section

This is Soldier's Hill today.

of the embankment. The woman was standing still, staring toward the Lightner monument. As the men discussed approaching the figure, she seemed to evaporate and disappear into the lengthening twilight.

In addition to reports of full-body apparitions, there have also been visitors that have heard the sound of a voice speaking or pleading into the wind near the bridge going to the old duck pond. Could this young woman, whose brief life ended so violently, still walk the grounds? Many in this town say yes, and that if one listens closely on a dark summer night one will hear a voice from the grave, lamenting her tragic fate. The voice of the Lady in White.

More Ghosts of Springdale

There are other mysterious tales of Springdale in addition to the Lady in White. The cemetery has areas with colorful epitaphs such as Mount Auburn, Mount Hope, Mount Sinai, and Last Supper. Soldier's Hill has the graves of over 300 Civil War veterans and was overseen by the statue of a weary Union soldier leaning on his musket. The limestone and marble statue at the center of Soldier's Hill was unveiled on May 30, 1870. The base of the statue is inscribed with the words "Liberty," "Justice," "Equality," and "Pro Patria." At the time of its construction, it was said the statue could be seen from all areas of the cemetery. In 1977, vandals toppled the statue to the ground. The statue was eventually restored and overlooks Soldier's Hill today.

There have been many reports of strange sights in the area of Soldier's Hill. One visitor the author spoke with told of an eerie encounter with a group of friends in 2002. She had heard the stories of the cemetery and had gone to the graveyard late at night with the hopes of seeing the apparition of the dead soldier. She and her friends went up to Soldier's Hill and sat down near one of the tombstones. As they sat there quietly talking, the group noticed a strange green mist that started near one of the tombstones. They commented on this, remarking on how the humid weather must have caused the strange color. As they watched, the green mist began to expand and grow, curling around the tombstones in the area and rising to a height of about six feet. They walked over to examine the strange phenomenon, but as they approached they just as quickly stopped again. Standing in front of them, about 12 feet away, was the figure of a man next to one of the tombstones. He had a thin, gaunt figure and was dressed in full Civil War regalia of the Union army, complete with jacket and cap. He did not appear as a solid figure but seemed to waver in the late-summer heat. She described him as having dark hair and a dark beard. As they stood and stared, the figure turned its head toward them and gazed at them fixedly with a vacant gaze. Terrified, the girls remained rooted to the spot, and as they watched the figure disappeared as quickly as it had come, becoming part of the strange green mist. The group wasted no time in hustling out of the cemetery and kept looking back to make sure they were not being followed. But the green mist they had observed had also disappeared, leaving Soldier's Hill in peace and darkness.

Another spirit that is said to roam Springdale is the ghost of a young girl. She appears wearing a late-19th-century dress with a white pinafore and is said to pop up from behind the tombstones to playfully frighten visitors. The child is most often seen in the Mount Hope section of the cemetery and appears to engage in an eternal game of tag. Her childish laughter is often heard darting in and out among the tombstones.

Not all the ghosts in the cemetery are human. The old pet cemetery was located at the site of the caretaker cottage near Perry Avenue. The cemetery was later moved, and the animals interred at the site of present-day Pet Haven. However, not all the animals rest in peace. The ghost of a German shepherd is said to haunt the area of the old pet cemetery near the caretaker cottage. The dog is a protective presence at the cemetery and appears late at night in a white, hazy glow, rushing at any intruder that is foolish enough to trespass on cemetery grounds. The animal disappears as quickly as it materializes, leaving those warned to make a hasty exit from the area.

In addition to the reports of spirit orbs, photographs taken at the cemetery often reveal white, misty shapes although the days when the photographs are taken are clear and nothing can be seen to the naked eye. These shapes can appear even on a bright, sunny day. Many other visitors have also reported seeing strange mists and shapes in the area, as well as gusts of icy cold air that issue from nowhere, even on a balmy day.

Springdale Today

Springdale Cemetery went through a long period of neglect and vandalism, in addition to mismanagement and exploitation by former trustees. The Springdale Historic Preservation Foundation was organized by concerned citizens to save the cemetery. In 2003, the City of Peoria, Peoria County, and the Peoria Park District signed the Springdale Cemetery Intergovernmental Agreement, and the city is actively involved in the management and preservation of this historic site. The cemetery is a beautiful and fascinating area, with acres of tombstones and mausoleums set among the rolling green hills. For those with a more practical interest in the site, over 50,000 graves remain available for sale, providing the intrepid history buff a unique opportunity to preserve a place in Peoria's history.

Christ Episcopal Church and Stone Church Road

Traveling down Farmington Road in Limestone Township, a visitor could enjoy the view of picturesque farmhouses tucked away among the gently rolling cornfields. A large stone church rises starkly from the local farmland, sitting silently on a hill and surrounded by tombstones. Christ Episcopal Church is located at 1604 North Christ Church Road between Farmington Road and Route 116.

In the summer of 1834, a group of English settlers, led by the Reverend Palmer Dyer, met to form a parish. They had emigrated from England and settled in Jones Hollow (present village of Norwood). The group held services in the home of Reverend Dyer but soon concluded that they should form their own church. To this end, the members contacted Bishop Philander Chase, who accepted the congregation into the diocese of Illinois in 1836. In 1837, Bishop Chase met with the settlers at the home of John Benson. Bishop Chase advised them of the importance of finding a place of worship. The settlers attended church at Robin's Nest, the residence of Bishop Chase, or at Jubilee Chapel, but were determined to build their own church.

John Pennington donated two acres of land in Limestone Township for the construction of a church and cemetery. The parishioners wrote to family and friends back in England in an attempt to raise money for the construction of the church. Funds for the building included a donation from the dowager Queen Adelaide of England, mother of Queen Victoria.

The erection of the new church began in 1844 and was finished the following year at a cost of $1,500. The timbers were hand sewn and pegged, and the walls are of sandstone from quarries near Joliet. The limestone used for construction of the church came from local quarries. Cypress and oak were donated, and the stained-glass windows were brought from England. The cornerstone was laid on May 17, 1844. On December 10, 1845, the church was consecrated by Bishop Philander Chase, Episcopal bishop of Illinois and the founder of Jubilee College. The bell tower was added to the church in 1889 and was made from stone taken from the house of John Flatman.

The church was busy and active, with over 100 parishioners in 1837. However, the membership gradually declined in the early 1900s as families moved away from the area, and by 1924, regular church services had ended. In 1937, a group formed to restore the church, headed by the Harry Stone family of Peoria. In 1960, the church was reopened with the assistance of St. Paul's Church in Peoria. The church remains a parochial chapel of St. Paul's Episcopal Church and was added to the National Register of Historic Places on February 10, 1973.

Christ Episcopal Church still features its original 1844 interior.

Christ Episcopal Church is home to many restless souls.

The church remains intact since its construction in 1844. The light-colored limestone building rises majestically from the rolling hills of the prairie, with five beautiful stained-glass windows gracing the interior. The interior of the church remains unchanged as well, with the original black walnut pews with hinged pew doors, dark red cherry wood baptismal font, and oil lamps suspended by iron hooks hanging from the beamed ceiling.

The countryside surrounding the church remains unchanged as well, with cornfields dotting the gently sloping hills and a small road running in front of the church. Despite the serene beauty of the scene, there are many reports of supernatural and paranormal activity in the area.

The Ghosts of Stone Church

There are many tales of ghosts that haunt "Stone Church." One lurid legend holds that a nun from the area was raped and went to the church to pray following the attack. She was so overcome by feelings of shame and guilt that she went up into the bell tower of the church and hung herself with a rope. Local belief holds that if one visits the church on a clear, moonlit night, one can see the apparition of the nun, still hanging in the bell tower, swinging silently in the night.

The most popular legend of Stone Church Road involves a farmer who owned land behind Christ Episcopal Church. The man's wife had died, and he was raising his only daughter alone. He thought the world of his daughter and was very protective, especially when she left the house at night. The farm road was unlit and very dark, with dangerous dips that could take a driver by surprise. The man frequently warned his daughter to be careful when driving at night. To combat this fear, he and his daughter arranged a special "safe" signal. Just before the car crossed the bridge near their home, the girl would instruct the driver to honk two short blasts, to let her father know they had arrived to that spot safely and would soon be back home.

One night, there was a particularly violent storm in the area. The young daughter had gone to a dance with her boyfriend, and the farmer paced the floor of their house, praying to hear the car horn that would signify her safe return. The girl's boyfriend had been drinking and was driving rapidly toward the small bridge where she was to give the safe signal. Instead, the car crashed, instantly killing the man's daughter and leaving her boyfriend unscathed. The man heard the car crash and ran out into the storm to find his daughter. When he came to the site of the crash, he discovered the body of his daughter.

The boyfriend, recognizing the man, started running down the road. The man, overcome with grief, ran back to his farmhouse and got his black car. He returned to the site of the accident and a short distance away saw the boy running down the road in the driving rain. The man gunned the black car, running the boy down and killing him. The legend goes that he then left the body lying in the middle of the road, where it was not discovered until the following day. There was insufficient evidence to convict the farmer of murder, and he never faced charges. Despite the lack of formal prosecution, the farmer began his own prison sentence, staying in his home and waiting for reckless or speeding drivers. He would then get in his black car and follow the drivers until they slowed down. There are also reports that he would also stand in the middle of his field holding a loaded shotgun, as a lesson to people to slow down on the road. Legend holds that even in death, the man stands watch with his gun and will wait for the safe signal from the bridge. If a car fails to give the signal, the man will rush at the car and then stand at the windows and stare at the occupants.

Many visiting the site report an encounter with a gaunt, older man in his black car. He will follow cars down the road, staying close behind them and shining his yellow headlights into the backseat. The headlights and car will then just disappear as quickly as they have come. Others visiting Stone Church Road report the sight of a black car parked beside the road and a man dressed in a flannel shirt and jeans standing close by. The man will stand directly in the middle of the road, forcing cars to stop. When the car stops and the occupants get out to confront him, the man and his car simply disappear.

Although there continue to be rumors of satanic cults or Satan worship at this site, these appear to be no more than stories to frighten or titillate high school students looking for a thrill. But even without proof of these tales, Stone Church Road remains a rather intimidating drive. Those visiting the site are advised that much of the land surrounding the church is private property and not open to the general public.

St. Patrick's Church and Cemetery

In 1839, missionary John Blaise Raho came to the Peoria area and established the first Catholic cemetery. Most Illinois Catholics at that time had turned to farming and had set up small communities throughout the state. In Kickapoo, William Patrick Mulveny donated an acre of land for the purpose of establishing a Catholic church and cemetery and deeded the land to Joseph Rosati, the bishop of St. Louis. Father Raho, acting as Bishop Rosati's delegate, laid the cornerstone for St. Patrick's Church. This tiny stone church is the oldest extant Catholic church in Illinois.

The cemetery established next to St. Patrick's Church was used as the burial ground for Irish Catholics in Peoria from 1839 until 1842. The headstones there bear witness to that fact, with biographical information provided regarding the deceased's Irish heritage. In 1859, another six acres were added to the cemetery.

There was a unique burial custom at the time among the Irish Catholic community due to the location of the cemetery in Kickapoo, as recounted by Robert Barger, in his book *A History of the Catholic Cemeteries of the City of Peoria*. Immediately following death, the women in the surrounding farms would arrive to wash, dress, and lay out the body. The body was laid on a bed, table, or board set up on a platform, and a candle was lit in the room. A wagon and coffin would be summoned from St. Patrick's, and the body would be collected and arranged in the back of the wagon. The next morning, a funeral procession of carriages and horses from farms from around the area would form behind the wagon. The procession would then slowly make its way to St. Patrick's in Kickapoo. Once the body arrived at St. Patrick's Church, the coffin was taken inside where a long mass was held for the mourners. The body was then buried in the small cemetery next to the church. Following the funeral, the mourners would picnic on the grounds of the cemetery, eating elaborate boxed lunches that had been prepared for the event and washing down the meal with water or more fortified spirits. In the evening, the entire group would form a line of carriages and return to Peoria. These burials were a major social event in the church and brought the entire Irish Catholic community together in a celebration of faith. The events would take an entire day, up to 12 hours, and remained a tradition until the first Catholic cemetery was established in the city of Peoria.

St. Patrick's Cemetery and Church remain in much the same condition as at the time of their original establishment, and the site has been the subject of reported supernatural activity. The apparition of an old man carrying a lantern is said to appear in the cemetery at night. The man walks among the tombstones, holding up the lantern and apparently reading the inscriptions. The legend is that this is the ghost of one of the first occupants of the cemetery, an Irish immigrant who was murdered in his farmhouse. Following his death, his wife quickly remarried. Legend holds that the Irishman hunts the cemetery grounds looking for the grave of his wife. Those driving by the cemetery during the day have also reported ghostly sightings of groups of picnickers dressed in early-19th-century garb sitting on blankets among the tombstones. The figures vanish as quickly as they are seen, and those traveling by are left to wonder if their eyes are deceptive or if groups of mourners still meet at the church to celebrate the life of one of their deceased members.

Regardless of the accuracy of these claims, St. Patrick's Church and Cemetery are important historical sites and retain the original charm and natural beauty that first attracted the earliest missionaries. This site is worth a visit for those with an interest in early Illinois history or the establishment of the Catholic Church in the area.

This tombstone belongs to William Patrick Mulveny, one of the original land grantees to St. Patrick's Church and Cemetery.

Here is St. Patrick's Church and Cemetery today.

Five

SCHOOL TIES

Bradley Polytechnic Institute is a beautiful memorial, linking the sweet memory of departed life
with all that is truest and best in the elevation of humanity, through . . . the mind
and directs the hand in harmonious development.
—Oliver J. Bailey, first president of the board of trustees,
Bradley Polytechnic Institute (1908)

Lydia Moss Bradley and Bradley University

No history of Bradley University, no matter how brief, would be complete without an examination of the life of Lydia Moss Bradley. Lydia Moss was born in Vevay, Indiana, on July 30, 1816, the youngest child of Zeally Moss and Jenny Glasscock. Zeally had served as a quartermaster in the American Revolution and later returned to Virginia, where he served one year as a Baptist minister. He married Jenny Glasscock on October 28, 1790. Lydia was the youngest of their six living children. The family moved to Indiana in 1815. Lydia attended school in the kitchen of a neighbor, Mrs. Campbell. She was also taught domestic arts such as butter making, cooking, preserving meat, spinning, and weaving.

Zeally gave each of his children a farm of 200 acres when they reached age 18. Lydia and her sister, Nancy Chambers, shared a farm between them. Lydia invested in real estate at a young age and bought 40 acres in addition to her share and made a good profit on the sale. She would later use a portion of this money to purchase the land for Bradley University. There are reports that Lydia's father named her the sole heir to his estate upon his death, to the intense displeasure of her other siblings. Lydia would never forget this family acrimony and would later relate that she believed the death of all her children was due to a curse wished upon her by her brothers and sisters.

Lydia Moss married Tobias Smith Bradley on May 11, 1837, in Vevay, Indiana. Tobias was the oldest son of Judge Bradley, a circuit judge in Switzerland County, Indiana. Tobias had clerked at a store for a time in Vevay before branching out into business for himself. Lydia received $1,000 in gold from her paternal grandfather, Gregory Glassock, as a wedding gift. The couple lived with Lydia's parents in Indiana for a time but eventually moved to Peoria in 1847.

Lydia, Tobias, and their four-year-old daughter Clarissa arrived in Peoria in 1847. At that time, Peoria had 4,000 residents and was growing steadily. Lydia's brother William Moss had arrived in Peoria in the early 1830s and had been involved in a trading business along the Illinois River as the owner of various riverboats. He was also involved in distilling, real estate, farming, and mining. His large estate from the river to the bluffs would later become Detweiller Park. When Lydia and Tobias came to Peoria in 1847, William Moss gave Tobias the role of captain of a steamer he had acquired in St. Louis, and Tobias became a prosperous trader. William and Lydian acquired extensive farmland in the west bluff, including the subdivision known today as the Uplands.

As their business ventures prospered, Lydia and Tobias had repeated tragedies at home. Their daughter Rebecca died while they were still in Indiana, and shortly after coming to Peoria their seven-month-old son Tobias Jr. died on December 3, 1847. Next Clarissa, their four-year-old

Here is the Lydia Moss Bradley House today.

Here is the Lydia Moss Bradley House at 122 Moss Avenue in 1921. (Courtesy of the Peoria Public Library, Oakford Collection.)

daughter, became ill and died on December 19, only 16 days after the death of Tobias Jr. Mary was born on June 26, 1851, and died 10 months later in April 1852. William was born on March 16, 1853, living only two years before dying in August 1855. Lydia and Tobias bought a large plot in Springdale Cemetery, and the remains of their five dead children were buried in a beautiful site with a view of the Illinois River. Only Laura Bradley remained, and the couple fixed their hopes for a legacy on their young daughter.

In 1858, Tobias and William Moss built a large brick residence at 122 Moss Avenue. At that time, Moss Avenue was the seat of the powerful and wealthy in Peoria, and the Bradleys fit well into the neighborhood of whiskey barons and real estate tycoons. This would remain Lydia Bradley's home until her death. Tobias and William invested in the distillery, railroad, and sawmill businesses and saw their investments prosper with each year. Tobias also reopened the Peoria Pottery Company, which soon became one of the largest manufacturers of pottery in the United States.

Tragedy struck the couple again when their 15-year-old daughter Laura died on February 7, 1864. Lydia was then 48 years old, ready to become a grandmother, not mother to another child. Lydia would later donate land to the newly created Peoria Pleasure Driveway and Park District, with the proviso that the park should be named Laura Bradley Park in honor of her daughter. The park is still in existence today and occupies the western part of the original Bradley farm that was built around Bradley and the Uplands. Lydia never fully recovered from Laura's death and developed an interest in spiritualism and is said to have engaged in séances to contact Laura's spirit. It was also reported she continued to set a place for Laura at the family table until her own death in 1908.

With the loss of their last child, Lydia and Tobias turned their time, energy, and considerable fortune to business ventures and civic improvements. They were instrumental in the start of the Peoria Public Library, donating $1,000 and encouraging friends and business acquaintances to give freely. But the tragedies stalking the Bradley family had not finished. On May 1, 1867, Tobias was traveling in his carriage from Groveland to Peoria. He was later found kneeling by the side of the road, blood running down his hands and face. A doctor was called, and Tobias was moved to his home in Peoria. He lapsed into a coma and died on May 4 without regaining consciousness. The carriage he was using was later examined, and it was determined that an axle had broken and Tobias had fallen onto the road and been fatally kicked in the head by the horse that was still attached to the carriage. He was only 56 at the time of his death.

Lydia Moss Bradley was left a widow with over 700 acres of valuable land and interest in numerous business ventures. After Tobias's death, Lydia traveled a great deal, gathering ideas for philanthropy. She visited Rose Polytechnic Institute in 1877, and this later became the model for Bradley University. She also visited the Chicago Manual Training School and Lewis Institute in Chicago. Although Lydia had only a limited education, she had common sense, keen business acumen, and a strong work ethic that would substantially increase the wealth of her estate.

Following the death of her husband, Lydia's philanthropic interest focused on providing a quality, affordable education to those students completing at least eight years of primary school. A site on the hilltop of Main Street in Peoria was chosen for her vision. On November 13, 1896, the charter for Bradley Polytechnic Institute was incorporated for the purpose of maintaining a school for both young men and women in the pursuit of arts, music, science, mathematics, ancient languages, engineering, ethics, and literature. The school would evolve from an academy into a four-year college and would eventually offer a graduate program.

The ground for Bradley Hall was broken on April 10, 1897, and classes began while the hall was still under construction on October 4, 1897. Textbooks would be provided free of charge to the 105 incoming students. The fee for incoming students was $20 per quarter or $60 per year, with scholarships available to those students who could not afford tuition and were deemed academically deserving. At its inception, Bradley Polytechnic consisted of two buildings, Horology Hall and Bradley Hall.

Founders Day was set for October 8, 1897. The event generated great excitement in the Peoria community and educational circles throughout the state of Illinois. Lydia had chosen red and white as the colors for Bradley after observing a centerpiece of red and white carnations at a trustee dinner. Lydia presented the keys to the school to the president of the board of trustees, O. J. Bailey. Lydia was dressed in her trademark black silk gown and had tied all the Bradley keys together with red and white ribbons. Following the ceremony, Lydia opened up her home on Moss Avenue for a general reception, replete with potted palms, elaborate buffet, and an orchestra. There was only one graduate the first year in 1898, but the ceremony and dignity that accompanied the graduate would set the tone for thousands of students following in those early academic footsteps.

In the early days, the students and faculty enthusiastically set about forming clubs and organizations. Night school programs were added in 1897. A dramatic club was formed in 1898. The first baseball team was also organized that year, and a football team started in 1899. Basketball began in 1904, when Bradley was still called Bradley High School. The first issue of the Bradley school paper the *Tech* came out on February 1, 1898. The paper later became a school newspaper, the *Bradley Tech*, which eventually evolved into the *Bradley Scout*, the name used today. A summer session was started in 1904, with total attendance of 55 students.

As Bradley grew and prospered, Lydia remained actively involved in management of the college and her many business interests. Unfortunately, her health began to decline. She had been battling cystitis since 1900, which resulted in periods of debilitating pain. On December 27, 1907, Lydia sent for her personal physician Dr. A. L. Corcoran to her family home at 122 Moss Avenue. Lydia's advanced age, combined with exhaustion and constant pain, finally took its toll. From the time of her illness in December until her death in January, Lydia knew that she was nearing the end of life. She developed lung inflammation and influenza. Despite all her pain, Lydia refused opiates, preferring to keep her mind clear. She called in her attorney and gave directions for the administration of her estate. She lapsed into a coma and did not regain consciousness. Lydia Moss Bradley died on January 16, 1908, at 7:15 a.m. in her own bed as the sun was rising. She was 92 years old.

Lydia Moss Bradley was a careful and efficient woman who left nothing to chance. In order to avoid any chaos or disruption of class schedules, Lydia had executed a warranty deed in May 1899 to Bradley Polytechnic Institute, conveying the entirety of her estate to that entity but allowing for a life estate and 100 percent of all profits until her death.

Lydia had drafted plans for her funeral in 1906, and her attorneys ensured the event was as Lydia had envisioned. A wake was held at her home on January 18, 1908, from 10:00 a.m. to 12:00 p.m. with watch provided by an honor guard of students. The coffin was draped with a blanket of white carnations, four inches deep, with the letters BPI spelled out in red. The bell at city hall chimed 92 times to represent every year of her life. The burial followed at the Bradley family lot on Mount Prospect at the Springdale Cemetery. Lydia requested to be laid to rest in a spot that was abundant in sunshine, and the grave site on Mount Prospect was bright and sunny, with an excellent view of the Illinois River valley. At the cemetery, there were mounds of floral offerings from businesses, education groups, and citizens from all over the state. As her coffin was lowered into the ground, the sun shone brightly on the banks of flowers. It was a fitting tribute to such a well-respected and successful woman.

The legacy of Lydia Moss Bradley continues in the advancement and expansion of Bradley University from a junior academy into a full-fledged four-year institute of higher learning. A graduate program furthers the work started by Lydia in developing academic minds and producing useful and productive members of society. Even today, Bradley University abides by a clause in

This statue of Lydia Moss Bradley greets visitors to Bradley Hall.

Lydia Moss Bradley its at her home on Moss Avenue. (Courtesy of the Peoria Public Library, Oakford Collection.)

Bradley University's Hartmann Center and Bradley theater are said to be haunted.

Lydia's will that states, "There shall be appropriated and used annually from the income of said Bradley Fund a sufficient amount of money to be expended by contract with some florist, or otherwise, for the purpose of once in each week during the season of flowers, decorating each of the graves in my lot in Springdale Cemetery with a bouquet of flowers and placing annually on Christmas Eve on each of said graves a wreath of evergreen, and appropriately decorating the same on the usual annual Decoration Day."

Bradley University

Bradley University continued to expand following Lydia Moss Bradley's death. Bradley Academy or Bradley High School was finally phased out at the close of the 1921–1922 school year, and Bradley became a standard four-year college. With the start of World War I in 1915, the Bradley Polytechnic Institute helped train a number of soldiers at Camp Bradley, an army school of mechanics.

Peoria embraced its hometown college, with citizens and businesses contributing the majority of a $750,000 endowment in 1925. In an effort to reach out to the community, Bradley held a series of public education lectures that were widely attended. The *Bradley on the Air* radio program ran from 1925 to 1938. A new library, funded by local endowments, was built in 1948.

Athletics played an important role at Bradley. In its early history, the names Techsters, Hilltoppers, Fighting Indians, Robbie's Fighting Indians, and Bradley Indians were all used for Bradley athletic teams. Bradley Braves came into popular use under the direction of coach A. J. "Robbie" Robertson, who served at Bradley from 1920 to 1948. During this time, the "Famous Five" played for Bradley: Les Getz, Carl Schunk, Dar Hutchins, Chuck Orsborn, and Ted Panish.

The school also had its share of hardship. In the summer of 1951, at least three Bradley basketball players were accused of taking money for "shaving points" in games during the 1950–1951 basketball seasons. There were indictments in New York, and charges of impropriety were leveled against president David Owens. In the ensuing scandal, three players pled guilty to conspiracy charges and were given suspended sentences. In December 1952, Bradley was voted out of the Missouri Valley Conference, even though its resignation had previously been submitted in June 1952. President Owens resigned on January 1, 1953. Bradley weathered the storm and remained a fully accredited university. The basketball team eventually rebounded, and a bid was accepted to again play in the National Invitational Tournament in New York City in 1957.

By 1957, Bradley University had 23 educational buildings, 156 instructors, and 4,349 students and was offering more academic, athletic, and social opportunities to its students then ever before. The college suffered a significant setback in 1963, when Bradley Hall was destroyed by fire. The fire started in the basement room under the chapel and gutted almost the entire building. The origin of this fire remains a mystery to this day. As a large crowd gathered to watch the flames eat away the building Lydia Moss Bradley had watched during construction, then president Dr. Van Arsdale received a telegram from Louis B. Neumiller, former president of Caterpillar Tractor Company, who pledged $75,000 for rebuilding Bradley Hall. Following the rebuilding, enrollment at the school steadily increased, reaching 6,100 students and 364 faculty by 1970.

Although enrollment would fall slightly as the school overcame a period of student unrest and faculty reductions in the 1970s, the college emerged stronger and more united. The Black Student Alliance was formed, with members calling for and organizing a Black Culture Week in 1969. The Bradley University Faculty Club was formed in 1972.

PEORIA'S HAUNTED MEMORIES

Ghosts of Bradley
Following the death of Lydia Moss Bradley, there were continued reports of her presence at her home on Moss Avenue. During her life, Lydia purportedly had a keen interest in spiritualism, and many of her neighbors reported that she held séances to contact the spirit of her dearly departed daughter, Laura Bradley. A nephew of Lydia's who had lived with his aunt while attending Bradley Polytechnic Institute continued to stay there after her death. He frequently heard the sound of Lydia's cane descending the main staircase as he had so often heard during her life. This was often associated with the strong smell of roses, Lydia's favorite flower. Visitors to the home continued to report seeing an apparition of Lydia herself walking in the area of her beloved rose garden, dressed in her traditional black silk gown with a ruffled front and wide black belt cinched with a silver buckle.

Regardless of the veracity of these claims, the presence of Lydia Moss Bradley is still clearly felt in Peoria by those attending Bradley University or enjoying the beautiful vistas in Bradley Park.

Meyer-Jacobs Theater
The Hartmann Center was originally built as Hewitt Gymnasium in 1908 at a cost of $75,000. The gymnasium was completed in the fall of 1909, and it was regarded as the finest facility in Illinois of its kind outside Chicago and the third-largest gymnasium in the nation. There were bowling alleys, pool tables, and an indoor track of 26 laps to the mile running above the main floor. There was ample seating for basketball games, and sporting events were held at the gymnasium until 1925. A swimming pool was built on the ground floor that today is part of the orchestra pit. The Hartmann Center was renovated in the 1970s, changing from a gymnasium to a theater and art gallery. H. W. (Jack) and Mary C. Hartmann contributed $500,000 for the renovation of the old gymnasium into the Hartmann Center. Today the Hartmann Center is home to Meyer-Jacobs Theater, Hartmann Center Gallery, and offices for the Department of Theatre Arts. It is also reportedly home to at least three different ghostly entities: a young boy, a former theater patron, and a "Lady in White."

According to legend, a young boy drowned in the pool in the basement of the old gymnasium, beneath the site of the present-day orchestra pit. The boy is said to be heard sobbing beneath the floorboards of the pit and scratching against the wood as he tries to get out of the water.

The Lady in White is a former opera singer who roams the backstage of the Meyer-Jacobs Theater. She is a reportedly a protective presence, watching over actors and productions to ensure that no one is hurt. Some of the female actors have reported the feeling of a cold, strong hand stroking their hair prior to a performance. In the 1980s, high-heeled footprints mysteriously appeared in sawdust that had been spread behind the theater curtain. The Lady in White will also turn out lights at the theater if rehearsals run too long.

The final ghost of the theater is the so-called "Brown Man." The Brown Man is a former regular patron of the theater who regularly attended performances, dressed in his characteristic dark brown suit. The Brown Man would sit at the back of the theater and keep an eye out for those talking or sleeping during a performance. The Brown Man was never afraid to issue a sharp reprimand to those in attendance to pay attention to the show. Following his death, many sitting at the back of theater have reported seeing the apparition of a man in a brown suit. He appears after the curtain has gone up and seems to be watching the show. The Brown Man is accompanied by the pungent smell of cigars. Even in death, the Brown Man continues to provide reminders to pay attention to the stage.

78

Tobias and Lydia Moss Bradley are buried at Springdale Cemetery.

Here is Bradley Polytechnic Institute in 1897. (Courtesy of the Peoria Public Library, Oakford Collection.)

Here is Constance Hall at Bradley University.

The corner tower of Harper/Wycoff dormitory is home to some restless spirits.

Sisson Hall

Sisson House was built at 410 Bradley Avenue in 1915. The dormitory was originally called Laura Cottage, named after Laura Bradley, and was mainly used for housing the wives of servicemen who were stationed at Bradley during World War I. In 1931, the name changed to the Greenhouse, and the building was used as a freshman men's dormitory. In 1946, the name changed again, this time to Sisson House in honor of Edward Sisson, the first director of Bradley Polytechnic Institute. Sisson was elected to his post on February 25, 1897. He had formerly founded the South Side Academy in Chicago and was only 29 years old when he assumed his new post in Peoria. Sisson resigned in 1904 after seven years of providing outstanding leadership and guidance to new students at the school.

Sisson Hall was remodeled in 1949 and became a women's dormitory. In the 1980s, it was converted into administrative offices. Soon after the building was converted, a student, Roberta Jones, hung herself during spring break in the women's bathroom of the third floor. The college was virtually deserted at that time, and in a grisly twist Jones's body was not discovered until students returned 12 days later. She was reportedly found still hanging in a shower stall. It is rumored her spirit has never left Sisson Hall. There are frequent reports that the sound of water running can be heard in the third-floor bathroom, and when investigations are made, the source of the sound cannot be located. Visitors also complain of a foul and mysterious odor on the third floor, like that of decaying flesh.

Constance Hall

Constance Hall was originally built as Bradley's first female dormitory in 1930 and was named in memory of Jennie M. Constance, who was head of the English department from 1919 until 1928. During the summer of 1928, Constance was studying for her doctorate degree at Northwestern University in Evanston. While walking back to her room from the university library, Constance was struck down and robbed two blocks from her residence. Constance died later that year from her injuries. In order to commemorate her service to Bradley, various women's clubs in Peoria raised money to build a women's dormitory in her honor. A site on College Avenue was chosen for the dormitory, and a cornerstone ceremony was held on November 24, 1930, with dedication of the building on June 9, 1931. By 1936, there were 21 girls living at the dormitory, and those residing there had a reputation for "good times."

Constance Hall is reportedly haunted by the ghost of Olive White, a former dean at Bradley in the 1950s. White was efficient and strict, enforcing curfews and keeping an eye on the young ladies in the dormitories. Her spirit is said to roam the halls of the dormitory, and her sharp heels can be heard clicking up and down the empty corridors late at night. Many have heard the footsteps and upon investigation have been unable to account for the noise. White is a protective presence at the college, checking in rooms to ensure that all her girls are safe and accounted for. Constance Hall was converted to the university music building in June 1961, but White's spirit continues to occupy the site.

Harper/Wyckoff Dormitory

The Bradley Home for Aged Women was built by Lydia Moss Bradley in 1885 at 2213 Main Street. The building was expanded in 1948, rebuilt into a men's dormitory, and renamed Wycoff Hall. In 1906, a new wing was built onto Wyckoff Hall called Harper Hall. A Main Street wing was completed in 1951, and the dormitory had the capacity to house 441 male students. The Harper/Wyckoff dormitory is named after Dr. Charles T. Wyckoff, a member of the first faculty at Bradley Polytechnic Institute, founder of the Bradley Historical Society, and honorary pallbearer at the funeral of Lydia Moss Bradley; and Dr. William Rainey Harper, first president of the faculty and enthusiastic promoter of Bradley athletics.

Peoria's Haunted Memories

The Harper/Wyckoff dormitory is said to be haunted by the ghost of John T., a young music student who died in Laura Bradley Park in 1987. According to legend, John T. had been drinking heavily the day of his death to celebrate the end of final exams. In his stupor, he decided to walk down to Farmington Road and continue his binge at the local bars. The story goes that while walking across a small bridge in Bradley Park, John T. stumbled over the edge, striking his head on the sharp rocks below and breaking his neck in the process.

John T.'s ghost is rumored to haunt his former dormitory, Harper/Wyckoff. His room was on the seventh floor, and often the elevator will take surprised visitors to this floor regardless of which elevator button they choose. The sound of uneven footsteps can also be heard echoing through the halls of the seventh floor late at night, the sound of John T. trying to get back to the safety of his dormitory room.

The Bradley University Library

The Bradley library was originally located on the main floor of Bradley Hall. However, as the school acquired more volumes and its student body grew, plans were made for a separate library building on campus. In 1948, final plans for the new library were made, and a groundbreaking ceremony was held on October 8, 1948. The building was dedicated on October 20, 1950. A new addition, which almost doubled the size of the original building, was added in the early 1960s. The library was originally called the Lincoln Library, but the name changed to the Shelby Cullom-Davis Library in honor of the donor of a $1 million gift. There are many ghostly legends of the library, including reports of cold spots, doors opening and closing of their own volition, and lights mysteriously turning on and off.

Bradley Today

Bradley University remains committed to its original goals of providing quality education and creating opportunities for the local community. Today Bradley offers its undergraduate students more than 100 programs. In 2009, Bradley University was ranked sixth among midwestern comprehensive universities by *U.S. News & World Report*. The picturesque campus is worth a visit by anyone interested in a quality education or the history of the area.

Six

RATTLING CHAINS

The old woman smiled, and answered in the same low, mysterious voice,
"It is the blood of Lady Eleanore de Canterville, who was murdered on that very spot
by her own husband, Sir Simon de Canterville, in 1575. Sir Simon survived her nine years,
and disappeared suddenly under very mysterious circumstances.
His body has never been discovered, but his guilty spirit still haunts the Chase.
The blood-stain has been much admired by tourists and others, and cannot be removed."
"That is all nonsense," cried Washington Otis; "Pinkerton's Champion Stain Remover
and Paragon Detergent will clean it up in no time," and before the terrified housekeeper
could interfere, he had fallen upon his knees, and was rapidly scouring the floor
with a small stick of what looked like a black cosmetic.
In a few moments no trace of the blood-stain could be seen.
—Oscar Wilde, The Canterville Ghost

The image of the haunted house has long held a place in local folklore and legend. Images of a dilapidated building with the shutters hanging askew and white shapes floating past the windows frequently appear in popular fiction. Many ghost stories revolve around a haunted house or building that is a center for supernatural or paranormal events. These buildings are inhabited by either deceased occupants or other visitors who in life formed a binding connection to the property. Most of the activity in a haunted house is related to a tragic or violent event.

The haunted house has its roots in ancient history, with the first notable ghost story related by Pliny the Younger. This story takes place in Athens in a large, empty house with a "bad reputation and an unhealthy air," where the ghost of an old man roams the halls at night. The old man is shackled and bound, and he rattles his chains in the darkness. The local people are afraid of the specter and refuse to spend the night in the house. Finally a philosopher, intrigued by the tales of the restless specter, rents the house and prepares to stay the night. Late in the night, the philosopher hears the clank of chains, and the sound grows louder and louder until the ghost suddenly appears. The philosopher follows the beckoning phantom to the courtyard, where it promptly vanishes. The next morning, the philosopher and local authorities dig up the spot where the ghost disappeared. There they find the bones of the man who had been shackled and chained. The philosopher summons the local authorities, and they remove the body and conduct a proper burial. Once he has been properly laid to rest, the ghost disappears. This ancient ghost story has provided the formula for countless tales written since that time. The ghost story continues to entrance audiences and provide subject matter for local folklore and myth.

During pioneer times, there was a firm belief that certain precautions had to be taken to prevent a home from inhabitation by evil spirits. It was believed that work on building a house should not be started on a Saturday or the spirits would cause problems during construction. Another common belief was that a gate should be built no closer than 15 feet from the front door in order to avoid bad luck. Many local builders held that a horseshoe should be placed in the brickwork of the chimney to prevent the entrance of evil spirits into the home.

Peoria's Haunted Memories

Peoria has its share of haunted houses, those buildings touched by the supernatural and plagued by stories of mysterious mists, roving specters, and strange noises. These tales are multigenerational and remain popular in local folklore.

The Pettengill-Morron House

Moses Pettengill was born on April 16, 1802, in New Hampshire. He married Lucy Pettengill in May 1833, and the couple moved to Fort Clark (later Peoria) in 1834. When the Pettengills arrived at Fort Clark, the population of the village was around 150. The downtown area boasted 30 log cabins and 3 frame houses. In 1834, Moses and Jacob Gale opened the first hardware and iron store in Peoria. Moses also became active in civic advancements as a founding member of the Main Street Presbyterian Church, a trustee of the village board, and helped organize the YMCA. Moses also helped establish the American Pottery Company in 1859.

In addition to their civic involvement, Moses and Lucy were interested in social reform. The couple was heavily involved in the abolitionist movement and founded the Peoria Anti-Slavery Society. Abolitionism was divisive and not a widely popular idea at that time, and the Pettengills risked the censure of their friends and colleagues in their work. The first Pettengill house at the intersection of Jefferson and Liberty Streets was a station on the Underground Railroad, providing protection for escaped slaves who fled across the border into Illinois.

In 1862, Moses bought lots on Moss Avenue and constructed a house there for him and Lucy. Unfortunately, the couple's happiness was short-lived. Lucy died in 1864. Moses mourned her death but, as was the custom at the time, quickly remarried. He wed Hannah Brent in 1865. This was not the end of Moses's misfortunes, however, as later that same year, the Pettengill home was destroyed by fire.

Moses set about rebuilding the house and finished construction in 1868 at a cost of $12,000. The Pettengill-Morron house is a graceful brick mansion in the Second Empire style of architecture originally located at 464 West Moss Avenue (present-day 1212 West Moss Avenue).

The Pettengill-Morron house has a porch running the width of the house and open at the end in a porte cochere. The kitchen was originally in the basement but was moved into an addition on the east side of the mansion. The house has 15-inch brick walls, with 11 rooms as well as a full basement and attic. The home originally had marble fireplaces in all the rooms, but the dining room fireplace was removed at some point and replaced by a built-in china cabinet. The drawing room to the right of the entry was originally split into a front and back parlor, each with its own fireplace. The home was completely renovated in the 1940s with the addition of a modern kitchen and bathrooms.

Following construction, the house was used by Moses Pettengill and his family. They were one of Peoria's first families and often entertained at their gracious and well-appointed home. Moses died in the house in 1883. His wife Hannah died in the home a year later in 1884. The Pettengills are buried in Springdale Cemetery.

The Pettengill-Morron House has been host to six owners and was rented for a period of five years from 1941 to 1945. The residents are as follows: Moses Pettengill 1868–1892; Samuel Clark 1892–1901; William Jack 1901–1903; Charles Thomas 1903–1941; rented 1941–1945; John Boyd Stone 1945–1953; and Jean Morron 1953–1966.

Jean Morron

In 1953, construction was approved for an Illinois River bridge and highway through downtown Peoria. Jean Morron's home at 305 North Jefferson Avenue, the Morron ancestral home for over 100 years, was scheduled for demolition. Morron moved to the Pettengill home at 1212 West Moss Avenue in 1954.

Jean Morron was heartbroken at leaving her home on Jefferson Avenue and was determined to preserve as much as possible to bring to the new mansion. From her previous home, Jean brought ornamental iron fencing, brass hand railings, the silver "Morron" nameplate on the front door, marble mantelpieces, and gas-lighting fixtures. She also brought her entire family collection of fine crafted mahogany and rosewood furniture; much of which dated back prior to the 1830s when the Morron family lived in Pennsylvania. Jean also brought the family's antique collection: silver, Limoges and Havilland china, chandeliers, crystal, oil paintings, and oriental rugs. Jean Morron died in 1966, and at the time of her death, she left the home in the same condition as she so lovingly kept it during her life.

The Peoria Historical Society was granted possession of the Morron house in 1967 and opened the home to public viewings. The historical society preserved the home as Morron had left it upon her death. Since that time, there have been many strange occurrences at the Morron house, suggesting that at least one of its prior inhabitants may have never left their beloved home.

Volunteers report that items in the Pettengill home are frequently moved within a room or removed from a room altogether. A table is set in the kitchen with Jean Morron's china as she would typically have set the table for her morning meal. Volunteers report that the china or silverware is frequently moved about in the mornings after the house has been locked for the night. Perhaps the table was not set properly? Jean was fastidious in her manners and taste.

Jean was very particular about her antiques and their placement in the home. She banished a Tiffany stained-glass dragonfly lamp to the basement, deciding that it was not a good fit with the rest of the decor. She had decided ideas about her possessions. Tour guides are frequently frustrated when objects are not in their proper place during a tour; as they point toward the spot where an item once sat, there is nothing there to reference. One item that is the frequent victim of this type of mischief is an antique porcelain bedpan that is in the drawing room. This porcelain pan with red and white flowering is the frequent object of the impish force lurking in the home. It is frequently moved to a different position in the room and once was found on top of a bureau in the upstairs bedroom. Tour guides are frequently baffled by this, as they can conduct one tour with everything in its place and bring the next group in a short time later to find objects either moved or missing. Jean was very proud of her fine home and particular about the antiques—perhaps too particular when she sees something out of place.

During one group tour, a guide escorted the group from the second floor of the home via the back servant's stairs and into the kitchen. She finished the tour in the kitchen and then guided the group out the back door. The tour guide returned inside the home and walked into the dining room on the first floor. As she did so, she distinctly heard the sound of running water coming from somewhere on the second floor. Puzzled, the guide walked back up the main staircase. As she reached the top of the stairs, she noticed clouds of steam coming from the upstairs bathroom, located directly across from the staircase. She went to investigate the source of steam and stepping into the bathroom noted that someone had turned on the hot water in the bathroom sink at full volume. She was understandably alarmed as moments before there had been no water running and there was no one else in the house. She turned off the water and went back downstairs to await other visitors, leaving the bathroom door wide open. She was perplexed, and a bit annoyed, when a short time later she again heard the sound of running water. She proceeded back up the stairs and noticed the bathroom door at the top of the stairs was only slightly ajar, rather than open as she left it. She proceeded cautiously, convinced that an errant tourist had wandered into the bathroom and was occupying the toilet. She pushed the door open, and once again, the hot water faucet in the sink had been turned on full volume and the bathroom was so full of steam she could barely see to turn off the water. As she turned off the faucet and looked in the mirror above the sink, she was startled to see a dark figure standing

Here is the Pettengill-Morron House as seen after rebuilding in 1868. (Courtesy of the Peoria Public Library, Oakford Collection.)

The Pettengill-Morron House looks much the same today.

behind her. She hastily wiped the mirror free of steam, but the figure was gone. She was alone in the room. She hurried back downstairs and called a friend who stayed on the telephone with her until more visitors arrived at the house.

There are other spirits reportedly on the grounds of the Pettengill house. The home has a beautiful backyard, which is the frequent site of weddings due to the picturesque setting. Jean Morron's last pet, a German shepherd named Fritz, is buried somewhere on the grounds at the back of the house. There are reports of the sound of a dog whining and scratching at the kitchen door, but when the door is opened there is nothing there.

Jean died in 1966 and is buried in Springdale Cemetery. The Pettengill house remains virtually untouched since her death. There are personal effects, letters, and books throughout the home. Perhaps it is only natural that Jean believes the volunteers are keeping her home in order for her return. If Jean does inhabit the home, she is a distinctly benevolent and protective presence, keeping a watchful eye on her beloved china, silver, rugs, and furniture and ensuring that those entrusted with the care of the home do things according to her exacting standards.

Judge John C. Flanagan Home

Judge John C. Flanagan was born in 1806, the eldest son of John and Jane Flanagan. The Flanagan family moved from Philadelphia to Illinois and eventually settled on a large farm near Kickapoo. During a business trip in 1832, John Flanagan Sr. contracted typhus and died in New Orleans. Jane Flanagan was devastated at the loss of her husband and contacted her oldest son, John Jr., who was studying law in Pennsylvania at the time. He moved to Peoria in order to assist his mother. With the help of John Jr., Jane Flanagan was able to continue managing the family farm.

The Judge Flanagan residence is the oldest home in Peoria and is located at 942 Northeast Glen Oak Avenue. Glen Oak Avenue to Prospect was formerly known as Kellar Road and later Bluff Street. The road was originally a dirt track for horseback riders and carriages. There are several different versions concerning the acquisition of the land for Flanagan House by the Flanagan family. One story maintains that John Flanagan Sr. acquired the acreage for the house plus 600 acres from the local Native Americans in 1824, in exchange for blankets, trinkets, and beads. Another, less colorful, story maintains that after John Flanagan Jr. came to Peoria in 1834, he bought the 20 acres on the east bluff, including the site for the house, for $500. Regardless of how the family acquired the land, Judge Flanagan put it to good use, building an elaborate brick home in the American Federal style at the site.

At the time the house was built in 1847, the village of Peoria was a rough frontier town, consisting of seven frame houses and numerous log houses. The area below Flanagan House had been deemed Dublin and Flanagan's Gut, due to a runoff ditch from the bluff. The Flanagan home was one of the first brick homes in the area, and the grandest and largest in Peoria at that time. The home was commonly referred to as the "Mansion on the Hill" and the "Manse" by the local villagers. The foundation was two feet thick and built of limestone from Kickapoo Creek. Stone and glass were brought by riverboat from Chicago for the construction of Flanagan House, with lumber provided by local sawmills.

Built in the American Federal design, the Flanagan home has wrought-iron detail at the front and rear porches that came from France in 1852, including an ornate entrance gate. The house was built on the Illinois River bluff and commanded sweeping views of the village below. Originally guests would travel up from the bluff on a tree-lined drive that encircled the house. At the time of construction, the home had extensive grounds and a large wooded area used by the local citizenry as a park.

The kitchen was once located in the basement but at some point was moved to the first floor. When the home was built, the south side of the house facing the Illinois River was the original entrance. The front entrance was moved to Glen Oak Avenue in 1852, and the main entrance hall remains off Glen Oak Avenue. Flanagan House featured a freestanding or "flying" staircase at the entrance hall. The large central hallway had entrances at either end that could be opened in the warm summer months to create a crosscurrent. The house has 20 rooms with solid walnut interior finish. The floor joints are reportedly of walnut that is 4 inches thick by 12 inches wide. The walnut used was taken from trees grown on the farm and processed at a sawmill on the site. The nails used for the structure are square and individually poured into molds. Judge Flanagan built his own brick kiln on the grounds and manufactured his own bricks for the property.

Following construction, the house was occupied by Judge Flanagan, his mother Jane, his brother James A. Flanagan, his sisters Louisa and Letitia, and Louisa's companion. During his time in Peoria, Judge Flanagan was active in community and civic organizations and was instrumental in the construction of a deep canal on Morgan Street for drainage on the east bluff. He and his family hosted elaborate dinners and dances and kept an extensive wine cellar in the basement of the home to refresh their guests.

Judge Flanagan was a consummate gentlemen and particular dresser. He always wore a broadcloth Prince Albert overcoat and a tall silk hat. Judge Flanagan had sideburns, and his auburn hair was naturally curly and worn long down to his coat collar. Judge Flanagan was well liked and respected in the community. Even the local Native American population respected him, and in the fall and spring, they would erect their tepees on the Flanagan property to leave the women and children while they fished and hunted in the Mackinaw valley.

Judge Flanagan never married. He devoted himself to the care of his invalid sister, Louisa Flanagan, until his death. Louisa had swallowed lead paint as a child and remained in a wheelchair with the constant assistance of a companion. Letitia, Judge Flanagan's youngest sister, married David Maxwell, a business associate of her brother. Following the death of her husband in 1881, Letitia moved in with her sister and brother at Flanagan House. The three siblings enjoyed an active social life, entertaining with numerous parties and dinners. The family had a large collection of heirloom china, glassware, silver, and furnishings.

In its heyday, Flanagan House had frequent visitors as illustrious politicians, businessmen, and statesmen visiting the city often were invited to stay there. Abraham Lincoln was the most illustrious visitor at Flanagan House, staying in a guest room at various times during the Lincoln-Douglas Debates from 1854 to 1860. There is a plaque dedicated to his honor in the room where he stayed.

The family had bedrooms upstairs, with Judge Flanagan occupying the master bedroom. His sister Louisa occupied a bedroom with a large balcony where she could have fresh air on the days she was too ill to go downstairs.

Judge Flanagan occupied the house until his death on June 4, 1891. He is buried in Springdale Cemetery. He left his two surviving sisters, Letitia and Louisa, with title to Flanagan House. The two sisters died within months of each other in 1892, and the house passed to Letitia's only daughter, Louise Maxwell Williamson.

Since its construction, the house has been occupied by Judge Flanagan, Louisa Flanagan, Letitia Flanagan Maxwell, Louise Maxwell Williamson, Joseph F. Farber, Benjamin Koch, Fred Faber, and Lena Gray.

Mabel Morrill owned Flanagan House from 1923 to 1962. She and her husband, Dr. Frank Morrill, shared a passion for travel as well as the theater, and Mabel served as director of the Bradley School of Theater Arts and Speech. She and her husband also hosted Sunday night dinners, an occasion for the more illustrious members of Peoria society to share a good meal and the sparkling conversation of their hostess. Mabel was also one of the founding members of the Peoria Players Theater. As her love for drama grew, Mabel was able to establish a theater at Flanagan House and host her own productions.

Here is Flanagan House as seen in 1921. (Courtesy of the Peoria Public Library, Oakford Collection.)

This is the Flanagan House today.

Flanagan House was acquired by the Peoria Historical Society in 1962 at a cost of $15,000. Along with the home, the society also reportedly gained a few spirits that inhabit the site. The ghost of Louisa Flanagan is rumored to haunt the library where she would sit for hours, quietly reading or writing letters and enjoying the handsomely furnished room. One visitor to the house reportedly asked the guide who the woman was in the library wearing the long gown. Perplexed, the guide asked who she was referring to. The visitor related that during their tour she had seen a lady sitting in a chair by the fireplace reading a book and had presumed she was a reenactor for the afternoon tours. The astonished guide informed the woman that there were no reenactors that day, and both returned to the library to look for the woman but there was no one in the room.

The ghost of Judge Flanagan is frequently seen on the grounds as well, wearing his trademark overcoat and silk hat. One visitor reported seeing the apparition of a man wearing an old-fashioned overcoat and top hat standing in the main entrance hall. She was going to compliment him on the accuracy and grandeur of his costume but, upon approaching him, was shocked when the man turned to look at her and then disappeared before her eyes. The man had simply vanished into the empty hall.

Even if a visitor does not have an encounter with the supernatural, Flanagan House has plenty to offer. Although this house is a museum, the comfortable and convivial atmosphere invites the visitor to relax and enjoy. It is one of the oldest historical sites in Peoria and continues to attract visitors both for its past as well as spectacular view of the Illinois River valley.

Peoria Mineral Springs

Peoria Mineral Springs is a 14,500-year-old natural spring located at Spring Hill in the west bluff. In its early history, Peoria took its water supply from the Illinois River, and wooden cisterns were set up throughout the streets for the collection of rainwater. The remainder of the town was serviced by hand-dug wells. The first municipal system for water conveyance was established in 1833, when Stephen Stillman was given a contract to conduct water from springs near Jackson Street in front of St. Francis Hospital to the courthouse downtown. This was accomplished through the use of wood pipes, wooden logs bored end to end and placed two feet underground. The water conveyed was used to mix mortar for construction of the new courthouse. Despite its early success, the Stillman system soon proved inefficient to service the growing population.

In 1840, O. A. Garnett deeded the Peoria Mineral Springs and the surrounding area to Zeally Moss for the latter's contributions in the War of 1812. In 1843, legislation was passed to charter the Peoria Water Company in order to improve any spring within two miles of the corporate limits of Peoria. As a result of this legislation, a spring near Spencer Street was excavated and a reservoir erected. Water was conducted in two-inch lead pipes to Main Street. At the square downtown, a 15-by-12-foot cistern was erected for use in the many fires that ravaged the early downtown area. At that time, the population of the town was 2,700 and increasing rapidly.

In 1843, Illinois governor Thomas Ford granted a charter to Norman Purple, A. O. Garrett, Charles Oakley, Lester Hurlbert, and William Moss to establish a freshwater supply for the growing city of Peoria. The Peoria Water Works Company was established on Martin Luther King Jr. Drive (formerly Seventh Avenue), across from the Peoria Mineral Springs. A brick reservoir was built into the hillside of Peoria's west bluff to contain the three natural springs that flowed at the site. Pipes were laid to carry the water up to two miles from the site. These fresh springs would provide the main source of water for the city of Peoria until approximately 1858. The site also manufactured ginger ale, peach cider, Rosy Malt, and Lithia Seltzer.

The cavelike brick reservoir was built into the hillside of the historic west bluff in 1843, featuring brick arches and a barrel-vaulted ceiling. It remains located in the bluff just below Moss Avenue and above Martin Luther King Jr. Drive. The reservoir was built for Peoria's first water company to capture the flow from the three springs at the site, and these springs continue to flow to this day. The reservoir goes back 140 feet into the hillside. The overflow from the springs was used to help supply Goose Lake, formerly at the site of the foot of the bluff at Western Avenue and Main Street. At that time, the runoff from the springs was producing 432,000 gallons daily. Goose Lake was drained in the 1880s.

A plaque at the site reads, "This plaque placed by Illinois State Organization of the National Society Daughters of the American Revolution Mrs. Albert Triebel, Jr. State Regent This Sixteenth day of March 1983."

A brick two-story home was built into the side of the hill at then Seventh Street and Spencer Street, about 250 feet from the mineral spring. Zeally Moss built the house at 701 West Martin Luther King Jr. Drive for use as his personal residence and as headquarters for the newly established utility. Part of the hillside was excavated and fitted with brick retaining walls to create a loading dock for the mineral spring products. The hillside was also excavated for the creation of a garden at the home.

Adjacent to the house on the east side is the only remaining original cobblestone road in Peoria. The road was paved in 1886. The cobblestones were used for traction due to the steep incline of the road. The road was known as Spencer Street Hill for many years. This is one of only two original cobblestone roads remaining in Illinois (the other is located in Galena).

The Peoria Mineral Springs and the area surrounding it are purportedly home to a number of spirits. Prior to the establishment of the Peoria Mineral Springs, the site was a Native American village and campground, and artifacts can still be recovered from this area. There are reports of strange lights moving about the wooded area of the springs at night, and it is rumored at least part of this area is the site of a former grave site and sacred Native American ground. According to GhostsofAmerica.com, the ghost of a young air force pilot who allegedly murdered his young girlfriend remains at this spot, and his apparition can be seen at night as he frantically gropes in the standing water in the brick reservoir trying to find her body.

Pere Marquette

The early inns built in Peoria provided social contact and a protection for travelers along the Illinois River. Peoria's first hotel, the Travellers Rest, opened in 1825 on the riverfront between Main and Hamilton Streets. The double log cabin hotel provided barracks-style accommodation, and visitors were required to supply their own blankets. The menu consisted of pork products and grits, and the bar only offered whiskey. In 1827, Fulton's Tavern opened on Water Street. The bar was well stocked, and this became a popular watering hole for local businessmen and thirsty travelers. The hotel boasted three "boughten" beds and a set of "boughten" chairs. Fulton's Tavern was in operation until 1834. Later that year, A. O. Garrett opened the historic Peoria House, located on the northeast corner of Main and Washington Streets. The hotel had a ladies' parlor and bar on the first floor. At the time it was built, it was widely believed to be the finest and best in the state. The hotel was moved to a new building in 1840 and renamed the Planters House.

The population of the area continued to expand, and local business leaders and merchants quickly realized that the downtown area needed a grand hotel for use during conventions and seminars.

The Pere Marquette Hotel is one of the most dominant and impressive structures in the downtown Peoria skyline. The 14-story hotel was built in 1926, at the height of the Roaring Twenties and "Roaring Peoria." The hotel cost $2.5 million to build, an amount unprecedented at that time. It offered every modern convenience, including a bathroom in every one of its 288 rooms.

The Pere Marquette was designed by Horace Trumbauer of Philadelphia. Trumbauer used the famous Waldorf-Astoria in New York as inspiration in the design for elegant lounges and an impressive main entrance. The lobby level held the grand lobby and entrance, the LaSalle

Here is the Hotel Pere Marquette today.

Room, the Cheminee Lounge, and the cotillion room. The grand lobby was designed in the Gothic capital design with high-domed, decorated ceilings, bold columns, a marble staircase, and overlook at the mezzanine level with iron railings and elaborate detailing in brass. The hotel was designed with two painted murals. The first was originally located in the cotillion room and featured Robert Cavalier de LaSalle departing France in 1684. The second mural was placed on the wall over the elevator bank and depicted Jacques Marquette landing at the Pimiteoui Indian village in 1673. At the time the hotel was built, it boasted a private club in the basement called the Playground, where those willing to break the law could escape the restrictions of Prohibition.

The 12th floor housed the owner's apartment, or presidential suite, an impressive collection of rooms with intricate woodwork carpentry and cherry paneling. The suite had a secret compartment built along the bookshelf in the reading room to store liquor. There was also a closet that would open into a cabinet, and once opened, a secret button opened another panel that swung out and was used as storage for a bar. A fireplace in the suite also had a secret panel where the original owners kept a personal collection of liquor. This suite was allegedly used by the more affluent gangsters traveling through Peoria in its heyday in the late 1920s.

As construction of the hotel was completed, a sweepstakes was held in Peoria to name the hotel. There were over 20,000 names proposed, but the $50 cash prize went to a local woman who suggested Pere Marquette after Father Marquette, one of the first explorers of the area. The Pere had its opening night on January 5, 1927. The event was attended by over 700 politicians, religious leaders, and civic leaders.

During the 1950s and 1960s, the Pere was a conference mecca, boasting the most group meetings for a convention center outside Chicago. Remodeling at the hotel was conducted in 1961, 1966, and 1972 and continues to this day. In 1972, the Pere was purchased and for a brief time became the Peoria Hilton. It was restored in 1983 and given its original name. The Pere Marquette remains a vital historical and architectural landmark in downtown Peoria and continues to host cultural, civic, and political events.

A number of restless spirits are rumored to inhabit the grand Pere. During the hotel's construction in 1926, a worker reportedly fell from a supporting scaffold and broke his neck on the ground below. His restless ghost is said to inhabit the lower lobby where he fell. He appears dressed in his work clothes: faded gray trousers and a white shirt with work boots. He presents a uniquely grotesque appearance, as his head is said to rest at an unnatural angle as it appeared in death.

There are also reports that the 12th floor is haunted by the ghost of a woman dressed in a 1920s-era green silk dress. Allegedly, the "Green Lady" played host to one of the gangsters in the owner's suite and was murdered in the hotel by her jealous lover. Her body was allegedly stuffed into a utility closet on the 12th floor. She is said to wander the halls, accompanied by the sweet smell of the gardenias she wears in her hair.

Judge Jacob Gale House

The Judge Jacob Gale house is located at 403 Northeast Jefferson Street in downtown Peoria. The building was constructed in 1838 in the Greek Revival style and is the only pre–Civil War house remaining in downtown Peoria. The house was built within five years after the first downtown grid was completed and the original street system established. It is the oldest single-family dwelling remaining in the original town of Peoria (area adjacent to the central business district).

The home was owned by Judge Jacob Gale, who was a prominent businessman and public servant. Judge Gale attended Dartmouth College and arrived in Peoria in 1834. A popular story of the time held that Judge Gale walked part of the way on foot, from Detroit to Chicago. Judge

Gale entered the hardware business with Moses Pettengill in 1834 but sold his interest in the business a year later and used the money to study law. Judge Gale was admitted to the bar in 1837 and formed a partnership with Judge Onslow Peters. He served as clerk of the circuit court in 1844 and became Peoria's fourth mayor in 1849. He was commissioned circuit court judge in 1864. Judge Gale died in his home on Jefferson Street on October 20, 1900.

The Gale home consists of a two-story brick main block, with a rear wing and addition. The rear wing served as the kitchen with a cooking fireplace, which is still in place between the addition and rear wing but has been covered by cement on the outside and plaster inside. The home remains as the best example of a single-family home of the time period and offers the visitor a glimpse of Peoria's early history. The Judge Gale House was placed on the National Register of Historic Places in 1982. It was purchased and restored in the 1990s.

The site currently houses law offices and is reportedly the subject of much ghostly activity. Reports have surfaced of the sound of footsteps walking up the stairs toward the attic of the house after business hours, as well as objects being moved in the office area of the home. There are also reports of mysterious cold spots.

Seven

RAILROAD TIES

*The 10th of August, oh fatal day! / That lured our loved from us away, /
full of bright anticipation / of sights for them in store, / little thinking most of them /
should view their homes no more. / Fathers, mothers, sisters, brothers, / and children likewise, too, /
had said their last goodbye on earth / as the engine from the platform drew.*
—Sarah J., excerpt from "The Chatsworth Disaster,"
Peoria Weekly Journal, January 26, 1888

The railroad was once an integral and vital part of Peoria society. In 1869, the Central City Railway Company was organized and a single-track mule-operated railway line was constructed on Adams Street from Hamilton Street to South Street. In 1872, service from Rock Island to Peoria began over the Rock Island and Peoria Railroad. By the 1880s, Peoria was an important transportation center, connecting the central Illinois town with Chicago and the rest of the country. The railroad served as one of the only means of transportation prior to the construction of interstate highways and local airports in the 1940s. The railroad quickly became a popular choice of transportation by those seeking pleasure excursions at the end of the 19th century.

The Chatsworth Disaster

Nearly 700 passengers from Peoria took a rail pleasure excursion to Niagara Falls in August 1887, but the journey ended tragically when a burning trestle near Chatsworth gave way, plunging the heavy train into a shallow ditch where it caught fire. Eighty passengers were killed and 120 were injured. At that time, it was the worst wreck in the history of the American railroad.

The train left Peoria about 8:00 p.m. over the Toledo, Peoria and Western Railway. It was made up of 12 coaches drawn by 2 engines. The passengers paid $7.50 round-trip to see Niagara Falls. Two locomotives were on the head end to speed up the load. Supt. E. N. Armstrong of the railroad, his family, and guests rode in a private car hooked directly behind the engines. Inside the train, the sleeping cars, smoking cars, and chair cars ($2.50 extra, round-trip) were jammed with tourists. The trip to Niagara Falls was very popular and the train was at maximum capacity.

The train was speeding along at about 35–40 miles per hour when it crossed the Livingston County line shortly before midnight. The train stopped to pick up a group of passengers at Chatsworth and then proceeded down the line. About halfway between Chatsworth and Piper City there was a shallow ditch spanned by a wooden trestle bridge. The ditch was filled with dry timber and leaves. One of the passengers would later recount that he looked out through a window and saw the wooden trestle on fire in the path of the speeding locomotive. He leaped from the train and was unharmed. The engineer of the first locomotive was looking ahead and also saw the burning trestle. It was too late to stop, but the first engine safely crossed the 18-foot bridge. However, the weight of the first engine caused the burning bridge to collapse behind it. The second engine rammed into the farther bank. The cars telescoped into one another, with piles of debris crashing over the still-burning trestle and steam screaming out of the wreckage. The sleeping cars were not crushed in the melee but were badly shaken. The engineer's watch stopped at 11:54 p.m., the presumed time of the crash.

Most of the passengers in the forward cars were killed instantly, ground into the collapsed debris. Those remaining were in danger of being burned alive, as the fire that had continued to burn licked eagerly at the new pile of debris. The engineer on the head locomotive took one look at the catastrophe behind him and set his locomotive for a record-breaking run to the next town for help.

The survivors desperately dug into the dirt at the bank, throwing it by the handful onto the smoldering flames. They later extricated axes and buckets and used those to transport dirt to aid the firefighting effort. The cries of the wounded sounded around them, and as they attempted to quench the fire, they also sifted through the rubble to extricate the dead and dying. The night was pitch black, making the rescue attempt even more difficult. Many of the victims were horribly crushed or mangled. The dead were laid out in rows and covered with coats of the male passengers while all possible aid was given to the injured. The impact had thrown open bags and valises of the passengers, and the site was scattered with clothing, shoes, and pocketbooks, further adding to the chaos at the scene.

Word of the accident was not received in Peoria until nearly two hours later, and it was almost 7:00 a.m. before a relief train carrying doctors and nurses arrived at the scene. The wounded were taken to the Chatsworth station and then transported to the Chatsworth Town Hall. The Chatsworth Town Hall had been transformed to a makeshift hospital, and the Chatsworth railroad station did service as a temporary morgue. There were at least 16 dead taken from the site and 279 wounded. Most of the wounded were released to return to their homes.

In Peoria, the Rock Island depot was set up as a temporary hospital and morgue and began receiving bodies the morning after the wreck until the next evening. The dead were packed into coffins, the bodies surrounded by ice for preservation. When the trains arrived in Peoria, the ice was thrown away and the dead were unloaded. Some went out on other trains, but the large majority were set up in the freight room of the depot. Many heartbreaking scenes took place as friends and relatives passed along the rows of victims looking for familiar faces. Funerals for the deceased continued for nearly a week in Peoria and the surrounding communities.

As a result of the disaster, over 255 claims were brought against the Toledo, Peoria and Western Railway by the families of the injured and deceased. To its credit, the railroad acted promptly to compensate the families of the victims. The claims were all settled by January 6, 1888, at a cost of $300,000 to the railroad. An inquest was held at the Chatsworth schoolhouse on August 17, 1887. The town hall was unusable due to the mess left from the dead and wounded.

Eyewitnesses at the inquest reported seeing a fire on the Toledo, Peoria and Western track between Piper City and Chatsworth, approximately two miles out of Piper City and two and a half miles from Chatsworth. The railroad workers at the inquest reported that they had set fire to the grass and weeds in the area around the wooden trestle bridge and left it to burn. Railroad workers would testify at the inquest that the area around the bridge was cleared of grass and weeds, and none thought the fire would get to the bridge. However, some debris must have been left as the flames spread rapidly, setting fire to stacks of railroad ties that were lying by the trestle works. The bridge burned before the first train crossed it. The first sleeper was hung over the burning bridge. The coroners' jury deliberated three hours and returned a verdict against section boss Coughlin of gross criminal negligence in leaving fire burning across the track and failure to inspect the track. Toledo Peoria and Western was censured for failure to patrol the track.

Rock Island Depot

The Rock Island depot and freight house is located at 32 Liberty Street in Peoria, site of the present-day River Station and Martini's on Water. Construction of the building was started in 1899, with a two-story depot attached to a one-story freight house. The depot opened to much fanfare in 1900. The Rock Island depot was finished at a cost of approximately $60,000. The

This Harpers Weekly *print from August 20, 1887, captures the carnage of the Chatworth train disaster. (Courtesy of the Peoria Public Library.)*

Here is the Rock Island train depot in 1910. (Courtesy of the Peoria Public Library, Oakford Collection.)

The Rock Island depot is Martini's on Water today.

original building featured a clock tower in addition to the large brick building. The tower rose 118 feet and was the object of frequent lightning strikes. The upper part of the tower was removed in 1939. The original entrance to the building was through a small arched doorway in the tower, with two small windows set on either side. In 1965, a brick connection was constructed between the depot and freight house.

First-class train cars came through the Rock Island depot in Peoria on a regular basis. The Peoria-to-New York City trip took 29 hours and was very popular with the local people in the early 19th century, when railroad ruled the transportation industry. There were 14 railroads that provided service to Peoria by 1901, and the passenger rate was 3¢ per mile. A streamline train began service in 1937 on the Rock Island Railroad between Peoria and Chicago. Known as the "Peoria Rocket," it quickly became one of the most popular services at that time. The price to go from Peoria to Chicago was about $5.44 round-trip. The four-car train would accommodate 175 passengers. By 1949, there were only four trains remaining that were running to and from Chicago per day. The last run of the Peoria Rocket took place on January 1, 1979.

The depot today is the site of the Martini's on Water bar but retains all of its original features and architectural design, including stained-glass windows and the original entrance archway. The bar's owner, Marty Walgenbach, purchased the bar in 2003 and takes great pride in the original fixtures that have been preserved at the site, including 35-foot ceilings and a 13-foot mahogany bar. The bar also features the original c. 1891 railroad clock above the lounge. The marble from the floor of the original depot was taken and used for the counter of the bar.

The lounge area of the bar features the original Wells Fargo safe that was used by the railroad in the early 19th century. The lounge is also home to one of the ghosts at the site, a brakeman who was killed on the railroad during its construction and is said to still work at the building. The spirit manifests itself with the sound of booted footsteps sounding across the bricks, and a dark figure has been reported standing before the fireplace in the lounge, dressed in the original railroad garb of the 20th century: boots, dark pants, white shirt, dark suspenders, and hat. The figure appears holding a railroad lantern that slowly and silently swings back and forth. There have also been reports of the sounds of music playing after the bar has closed and circles of light that appear on camera. Mysterious cold spots often alarm bar patrons, and there are reports of voices raised in conversation in otherwise empty areas of the bar.

The Rock Island depot remains as one of the last representations of the important part the railroad played in Peoria's history. The City of Peoria acquired the Rock Island depot in 1976. In the 1980s, there was a revitalization effort in the downtown area, and a new restaurant, River Station, opened in 1981. Martini's on Water continues to serve the Peoria community and is worth a visit for a beverage and self-guided tour of the building's magnificent interior.

Whiskey and the Railroad

In 1880, the average American adult consumed 2.4 gallons of spirits annually. Whiskey was the liquor of choice due to its affordability and easy availability of local ingredients for production. With the rows of cornfields busily sprouting in the rich, black soil, it was only natural that early farmers in Peoria would examine possible uses of their surplus product. It quickly became clear that Peoria, with its abundant fields, central location, and position on the Illinois River, was the ideal spot to produce the "High Wine" the country demanded.

In 1835, Capt. Almiran S. Cole started Peoria's first distillery at the site of the Cedar Street Bridge. At that time, corn sold for 10¢ per bushel, and the bushel would produce five gallons of whiskey. The whiskey sold for almost 20¢ per bushel, providing the distillery with a tidy profit. Cole brought in consultants and construction workers from St. Louis to build his distillery. Cole sold the first company but in 1850 partnered with Tobias Bradley, William Moss, and Benjamin Bourland to set up a second distillery. More distilleries were quickly established, and by 1865,

Here is the interior of the Rock Island train depot as seen in 1930 and today as Martini's on Water. (Above, courtesy of the Peoria Public Library, Oakford Collection.)

Peoria had 14 distilleries running from State Street to Bartonville. From 1837 to the early 20th century, Peoria would be home to 24 breweries and 73 whiskey distilleries, earning it the moniker "Whiskey Capital of the World."

In 1888, the Distilleries and Cattle Feeders Trust or "Whiskey Trust" was formed. The trust was modeled after Standard Oil, and members sought to acquire the small-scale distilleries in an effort to control whiskey prices. Once it acquired these distilleries, the trust closed almost all of them down to limit production capacity. At its peak, the trust represented nearly 90 percent of the industry output in the United States. The trust was accused of a number of anticompetitive strategies, including intimidation and predatory pricing. A federal investigation ensued, with the end result the trust reorganizing as an Illinois corporation in 1890, known as the Distilling and Cattle Feeding Company. The trust entered receivership in 1895 and never regained its former market dominance.

In 1919, Prohibition, combined with a crippling drought, closed most of the distilleries in Peoria. A few remained in operation, producing for "medicinal" purposes under heavy federal government regulation and scrutiny. Following Prohibition, production resumed, and by 1954, the city was producing 200,000 gallons per day or 34 million gallons per year.

Initially the Illinois River was used as the primary means of transportation of spirits. Whiskey was easier to transport downriver than corn, and it quickly became Peoria's top export. However, with the advent of railroads through the area, manufacturers turned to the rails for quicker and easier transportation of their product. Corn and coal were two of the most important materials for making whiskey, and the railroad was indispensable in carrying these raw materials through Peoria.

During the heyday of the Whiskey Trust in the late 1800s, whiskey barons in Peoria built elaborate mansions on the bluffs overlooking the distilleries that lined the Illinois River valley below. High Street and Moss Avenue were in an area referred to as "High Wine," which was one of the most magnificent drives in Peoria. Illustrious residents of this area included Tobias and Lydia Bradley, William Moss, and Moses Pettengill. One of these mansions was the home of railroad magnate and antilabor activist George P. McNear Jr., owner of the Toledo, Peoria and Western Railway.

Toledo, Peoria and Western Railway

The Toledo, Peoria and Western Railway dates back to 1837, when money was appropriated to build a railroad line from Peoria to Warsaw. Eventually this idea was abandoned, but on February 12, 1849, the state legislature granted a charter to the Peoria and Oquawka Railroad Company to build a railroad from Peoria to the Mississippi River. An eastern extension to the Indiana state line became the eastern division of the Toledo, Peoria and Western Railway. The Toledo, Peoria and Western operated east out of Keokuk, Iowa, to Peoria, and west out of Peoria to Effner, a total distance of 239 miles. The rails were made of wood with strips of sheet iron nailed to complete the tracks.

George P. McNear Jr. bought the Toledo, Peoria and Western Railway on June 12, 1926, when he was just 32 years old. It was rumored he had walked the 239-mile line himself prior to bidding at auction. McNear was a 1913 engineering graduate of Cornell University. He had served in France at a railroad assignment with the army engineers. McNear bought the Toledo, Peoria and Western for $1.3 million at a foreclosure sale. He had certified checks for $65,000, barely 5 percent of the cost of the sale, but had confidence he could restore the rail line to profitability. At that time, the railroad had been losing between $15,000 to $20,000 per month. By McNear's fourth month of ownership, the railroad began to show a profit.

In 1940, an attempt was made by organized labor groups to unionize the railroad, and there were allegations that trainmasters were threatening employees to resist the union. An investigation ensued. McNear, president of the Toledo, Peoria and Western Railway, was arrested in January 1941 following a federal investigation. He was charged with attempting by threat and coercion to keep his employees from organizing a union in violation of the Railway Labor Act. He was arrested with two of his officials, H. H. Best, superintendent, and Bruce Gifford, trainmaster. The charges stemmed from intimidation and coercion against railroad employees in the summer of 1940.

McNear refused to arbitrate a wage dispute between the Brotherhood of Railroad Trainmen and the Brotherhood of Locomotive Firemen and Enginemen, and his threat to implement substandard wages and working conditions caused the brotherhoods to strike on December 28, 1941. The strikers contended a new contract proposed by McNear would have abolished seniority in job assignments and reduced wages. The management argued the new contract would raise average wages by 26.7 percent.

McNear refused to reconsider the wage reductions and other changes he had made to the detriment of the government. The workers appealed to Pres. Franklin Roosevelt, requesting he take over operation of the Toledo, Peoria and Western Railway to expedite shipments of war materials.

On December 7, 1941, McNear locked out nearly all employees who had placed a virtual embargo on all shipments. McNear hired a number of gangster thugs from Chicago to intimidate the strikers. There was gunfire on both sides as the confrontation turned bloody.

The Toledo, Peoria and Western Railway rested its case on January 15, 1942, and requested an injunction against strike violence. McNear testified that he had attempted to protect his company against property damage from any strike and that he authorized hiring additional armed guards but ordered them not to use their weapons. McNear testified he had attempted to request protection from local law enforcement but was either refused or was told he would be charged for the effort. McNear contended he needed protection for the moving trains from Indiana to Iowa.

McNear continued to refuse arbitration. The United States District Court issued an injunction against the national brotherhoods to prevent further acts of violence and interference with interstate commerce. On March 14, 1942, McNear rejected a request by President Roosevelt to allow the National War Labor Board to arbitrate the strike.

On March 22, 1942, President Roosevelt seized the railroad by executive order and appointed J. W. Barringer, associate director of the office of defense transportation railroad division, as "federal manager" of the railroad. The workers officially declared the strike over following federal seizure of the railroad. Barringer had instructions to reinstate nearly all of the 104 strikers under wages and conditions that were in place prior to the strike on December 28, 1941.

McNear continued to refuse arbitration following the federal seizure. McNear contended the brotherhood was attempting to prevent the trial of Paul Brokaw and two other brotherhood members set for March 23, 1942, on charges of conspiracy to dynamite one of the railroad's bridges during the three-month union dispute.

McNear and two of his aides were acquitted of federal charges that he tried to prevent his employees from organizing a local union on April 23, 1942.

The federal injunction issued to the railroad was reversed by the supreme court on January 17, 1944. On May 20, 1945, a federal judge ordered the government to return the railroad to McNear, finding the federal government was in violation of federal law.

Pres. Harry S. Truman ordered the Peoria line be returned to private control under the management of McNear on October 1, 1945. The union objected to the return to private control. D. B. Robertson, president of the brotherhood, urged President Truman to revoke the order restoring control to McNear until McNear agreed to negotiate with the union. Robertson contended that McNear intended to return all employees to rates, wages, and conditions that were in place prior to federal seizure on March 22, 1942. McNear contended he was making voluntary increases to wages, which would increase pay for all classes of employees, but would not negotiate. He argued that the employees had not been represented by the union prior to March 22, 1942, and might not want that representation upon their return.

Officials of railway union organizations planned a strike on the line as soon as the transfer of power was complete. It was clear that there would be a showdown on October 1, 1945, and many feared this would once again end in violence. A spokesman for the railway labor organization was quoted as saying a strike would immediately be called following transfer to the railroad back to McNear.

McNear announced on September 27, 1945, that in view of strike threats and rumors of violence that an embargo on all traffic would be in effect starting on October 1, 1945. McNear claimed there could not be a strike as there was no employment relationship between the workers and the railroad, since the people involved were the employees of the federal government. Despite McNear's protestations, the strike continued.

McNear claimed that on October 1, 1945, large members of the alleged strikers had unlawfully prevented the railroad employees from gaining access to offices, yards, and facilities. McNear continued to deny that a strike existed, claiming the people there were not his employees. McNear offered to reemploy some of the workers that were on the government payroll when McNear took over but specifically reserved the right not to hire 25 workers who he claimed had performed acts of violence against the railroad.

Violence erupted on Christmas day 1945, when a shot was fired at strikebreakers. On February 6, 1946, the railroad was running a train from Peoria to Effner, Indiana. Events of the day are controversial. The train carried over a dozen armed men, and a large number of strikers followed in their cars. There are different versions of the story. One was that the Toledo, Peoria and Western train attempted to run through picket lines, and the strikers tried to forcibly stop the train. A gun battle ensued. Another version is that the train stopped at a grain elevator at Gridley to switch tracks. As four of the armed guards got out of the train to throw the switch, the strikers hurled rocks and other projectiles. The four guards fired on the large crowd of strikers, killing Irwin Paschon of Peoria and Arthur Browne of East Peoria. Three other strikers, Amos Vinson, Russell Esslinger, and Howard W. Williamson, were injured. Howard Williamson would later recount he believed the first shot hit his leg and that the shot might have been fired on accident. However, when the first shot was fired, the guards opened fire on the strikers. Although the striking railroad workers denied they had any guns, Gridley residents testified that they had seen the picketers with guns both before and after the shooting.

Although the four guardsmen were charged with murder, a McLean County circuit court jury acquitted the men of all charges on March 24, 1946. Despite their vindication in court, the men were fired by McNear.

On December 6, 1946, a federal court injunction ordered 13 unions to stop interfering with road operations, and on January 10, 1947, federal judge J. Leroy Adair banned union interference with transfer of freight cars. McNear appealed to federal and local law enforcement officers for assistance, claiming that his men were being fired on in the East Peoria yard and freight trains continued to be derailed. McNear testified before a congressional investigating committee that the United States attorney general and FBI had refused to interfere with the violent practices of the union brotherhood in their campaign against his railroad.

Murder of George P. McNear Jr.

George P. McNear Jr. was a powerful, influential, and successful businessman in Peoria circles. He owned a large mansion at 202 Moss Avenue that had once belonged to Lydia Moss Bradley, founder of Bradley University. In addition, McNear owned a "farm" on the outskirts of Peoria

This 1947 view shows the path taken by George P. McNear Jr. after being shot. No. 1 is the shot site. No. 2 is where his body was found at the corner of Moss Avenue and Sheridan Street. (Courtesy of the Peoria Journal Star Archives.)

next to Mount Hawley Country Club. The farm occupied over 200 acres in the area that is now the Edgewild subdivision and was home to pigs, cows, chickens, and crops. McNear was an avid tennis player and built elaborate tennis courts on the farm, two inside and two outside. It was remarked that even in the midst of the violence and legal problems, McNear could always find time to talk about his tennis game.

On a cold, cloudy night on March 10, 1947, McNear attended a Bradley basketball game at the National Guard armory located at Hancock and Adams Streets. After leaving the game, McNear walked up Main Street to High Street, along High Street to Sheridan Street, and north on Sheridan Street toward Moss Avenue outside his residence.

Earlier in the evening, the power had gone off in the west bluff, due to a break in a major transformer. McNear's wife had been attending an Amateur Musical Club concert and went to bed when she got home. She reported that McNear's car was in the garage when she returned at 10:30 p.m., and she assumed her husband had gone for his customary evening walk.

McNear was walking one block from his home at 202 Moss Avenue when there were shots fired. McNear was mortally wounded by six shotgun pellets in his head and upper body. It was estimated the shooting took place at 10:40 p.m. McNear was rushed to nearby St. Francis Hospital, where he died on an operating table at 11:05 p.m. He was unable to speak prior to his death.

It was later determined that after being shot, McNear had attempted to return to his home at 202 Moss Avenue. McNear managed to stagger from the corner of Sheridan and Moss and crawl to the Leisy residence at 100 Moss Avenue, more than 100 feet from the scene of the crime. There were marks on a nearby tree, leading police to speculate that the murderer had hidden for some time, waiting for McNear to walk by. Wadding found at the scene indicated that McNear had been killed from a close range.

McNear was buried in the family mausoleum in Springdale Cemetery. His body was later shipped to Petaluma, California, where his father was living. As a tribute to McNear, all railroad operation was halted except that considered essential. The railroad offered $25,000 for the capture and conviction of McNear's murderer. An additional $16,155 had been raised by local businesses and contributed by private individuals. None of the reward money was ever collected.

Dr. Robert Sutton at 107 Moss Avenue claimed that he heard the sound of a gunshot at the time of the murder. An unidentified automobile was seen turning on High Street and fleeing at high speed. Another car, a 1936 Ford, proceeding without headlights, was observed by an eyewitness going from High Street down State Street (State Street is now closed to through traffic, but at one point connected High Street to downtown).

The police believed that McNear's assassin may have been trailing him for days, awaiting his moment to find McNear alone and unarmed. Police recovered some interesting clues at the site: a footprint, gloves, some wadding paper, six shotgun pellets, and license numbers from the two cars that had been spotted leaving the scene by eyewitnesses.

On March 22, 1947, a boy playing found a box containing Remington 00 shotgun shells behind a billboard at the corner of Knoxville Avenue and Lake Street. This was the same type of shotgun that had been used to kill McNear and the same size shotgun shell that had been used against the strikers at Gridley. There were two shells missing from the box.

No murder weapon was ever found, despite an exhaustive search of the grates and sewers in the neighborhood. Fourteen strikers from Toledo, Peoria and Western were questioned. The story made national news, and a crowd of reporters swooped down on Peoria, eager to get the inside story of the crime.

Three days after the murder, the FBI started its own investigation, claiming federal jurisdiction on the basis that McNear's civil rights had been violated by his being murdered. The FBI released

Here is the site of the George P. McNear Jr. murder at the corner of Moss and Sheridan Avenues. McNear was shot by the tree, stumbled across the street, and died by the X.

a list of the leading suspects in the murder; included among them were Howard Williamson and Charles Davis of Mossville, Williamson's uncle. Both men were also top suspects of the Peoria Police Department. Williamson was among five strikers shot by railroad guards in a confrontation at Gridley on February 6, 1946. Davis and his wife were also present at Gridley. Two of the five strikers died from their wounds. Both men were members of the railroad union on strike against Toledo, Peoria and Western. Both Charles Davis and his wife, Lucille, had been questioned repeatedly regarding the murder, and both refused to submit to lie detector tests. Williamson however, agreed to take the test, but it was never administered. FBI agents listed Williamson and Davis the only real suspects in the case a year and a half later. Williamson quit the railroad shortly after the strike was resolved, and Davis died in 1965.

There was a lack of cooperation between the Peoria Police Department and the FBI that many believed prevented the resolution of the case. Whatever the reason, there are many stories surrounding the murder of George P. McNear Jr. and the subsequent ghostly sightings in the area of his death.

The Haunting

The unsolved death of George P. McNear Jr. has generated much speculation and rumor. In 1980, the *Peoria Journal Star* newspaper filed a Freedom of Information Request with the FBI concerning the murder. In response, the FBI released 3,000 pages of records, most heavily redacted with many pages missing. The information that was released was instructive. Suspect Charles Davis, Howard Williamson's uncle, left his home in Mossville at 7:00 p.m. on the night of the murder and picked up Williamson at his apartment at 1121 North Madison Street in Peoria. Davis regularly carried a doubled-barreled shotgun in this vehicle. According to the pair, they traveled around Peoria looking for a poker game. Several witnesses claim to have seen them driving in a car the night of the murder.

The murder remains unsolved to this day, but frequent sightings continue to be reported on High Street in connection with the 50-year-old crime. Residents of the area report sightings of a ghostly 1930s locomotive that roars down the street with the lights off, only to mysteriously disappear at the end of High Street at the site of the McNear murder. According to local legend, the faint sound of a shotgun blast can be heard on the anniversary of McNear's death, and a shadowy shape has been reported to appear at the corner where McNear was murdered. Upon approach, the figure fades into the night.

Anyone visiting the area can clearly see where the murder took place and trace the path McNear took on his attempt to return home after the fatal shooting. Although the McNear mansion is gone, the scene of the crime looks remarkably as it appeared in 1947, and it is easy to see why these reports of ghostly activity continue.

Eight

SAINTS

*Oh, Mother, have you touched the mystic shore? / Then pray for us, as you have done before. /
The fervor of your prayer, so good and true / Will bless our lives, and all that we shall do. /
On earth, you have long been our guiding star, / Forget us not! Oh guide us from afar. / Upon
the unknown sea, so deep and dark, / May find at last, at last, a home in Jesus' heart.*

—Anonymous, "A Farewell Thought for Our Departed Mother"
written at the death of Mother Mary Frances Krasse

Early Medicine in Peoria

In 1844, Elias Cooper moved from Danville to Peoria to open a surgery. Dr. Cooper was only 24 years old but was energetic, ambitious, and eager to serve and educate the community. He opened an office in the center of downtown Peoria in a three-story building. The second floor contained the reception area, office, and examination rooms. Dr. Cooper turned the third floor of the building into an anatomical museum. His museum contained skeletons at various stages of human development, as well as some of the more interesting tumors he had removed. In 1845, Dr. Cooper opened a dissecting room in Peoria and gave lectures in anatomy as he dissected his corpses.

Dr. Cooper had an active practice, as bodies of deceased criminals were given to local physicians for scientific experimentation. This practice had been ongoing since the 13th century and was seen as a further punishment to the criminal and his family, as his body was stripped of all dignity and died a second death. This was also a way to prevent the despicable act of grave robbing, whereby many doctors sought to obtain corpses for experimentations. The Illinois criminal code of 1833 expressly provided for the delivery of hanged corpses to local physicians. Many opposed this practice as inhumane, and the citizens of Peoria were very suspicious of Dr. Cooper's activities in the dissecting room, suspecting that the cadavers had been recovered from local graves. Dr. Cooper quickly established a reputation in the city for cosmetic improvements to the citizenry, removing unsightly growths and other deformities. His demeanor and enthusiasm soon aroused jealousy among local professionals, and his enemies sought to end his dissecting practice on both moral and legal grounds.

The matter came to a head in 1850. In that year, a farmer and cattle dealer named Hewitt withdrew $2,500 from his bank. Thomas "Tit" Jordan was a thief operating in Peoria at that time and told Thomas Brown and George Williams of the bank withdrawal. The pair followed Hewitt home from the bank. Hewitt departed from his buggy at the bottom of the west bluff to spare his horses his weight on the trip up the hill. Brown and Williams accosted Hewitt and demanded his money. Hewitt refused, and the pair beat him with a wooden bat, fracturing his skull and rendering him unconscious. They then robbed Hewitt. They were frightened away by the approach of a group of teamsters up the bluff. The teamsters thought Hewitt was drunk and roused him and helped him into his buggy. Hewitt made it to a local tavern before he lost consciousness, and he was carried to his home. He died there nine days later.

Brown and Williams were spotted running from the scene of the crime, and a posse caught up with them as they sought to escape to Springfield. All the stolen money was recovered, found sewn inside black silk neckerchiefs the men were wearing. They were brought before Hewitt, who identified them as his assailants. They were found guilty of murder and sentenced to be hanged on December 20, 1850. However, a stay of execution was ordered so authorities could locate Jordan, the mastermind of the robbery. Angered by the delay, a lynch mob formed outside the jailhouse, easily overpowering the sheriff and deputies. The crowd captured Williams and dragged the already erected scaffold to the middle of the street. Brown was more fortunate; he had a bat that he used to strike down anyone entering his cell and thus managed to avoid mob justice.

Williams was placed on the scaffold, but the anger of the mob by that time had diminished, and no one would put the rope around his neck. He was returned to the jail to await execution. On January 19, 1851, Brown and Williams were hanged for the death of Hewitt. A gallows was erected on the open prairie, and the hangings were a public spectacle attended by over 10,000 eager spectators.

Prior to the death of Brown and Williams, Dr. Cooper had applied to the court for permission to have the bodies after death. After the hanging, the bodies were cut down and taken to his office in the middle of downtown Peoria and carried up the back stairs to the dissecting room. The community was in an uproar over the idea of the notorious criminals being dissected in the middle of the city. Dr. Cooper met the uproar with his usual calm and aplomb and was able to temporarily quiet his detractors. He proceeded with the dissections, adding some specimens to his anatomical museum and increasing attendance.

To assuage public sentiment, Dr. Cooper opened the first hospital in Peoria in September 1851 a mile from the edge of town. The official name of the hospital was the Peoria Eye Infirmary and Orthopedic Institution, but due to the doctor's dissecting practices it soon earned the name the "Spook House."

Despite the nickname, Dr. Cooper's hospital was very successful, and he soon had a large number of patients seeking care, both local citizenry and residents of Indiana, Iowa, and Kentucky who had heard of his expertise as an orthopedic surgeon. The Illinois legislature of the Anatomy Act of 1885 mandated that the body of any deceased person requiring burial at public expenses could be released upon request to a medical school or physician, provided that the relatives were notified and agreed to this disposal.

Dr. Cooper's contributions to the area continued until his death. By that time, the Spook House had developed the reputation as a haunted house, with tales of those that Dr. Cooper had dissected returning from the grave in search of the anatomical abstractions. The Spook House was later closed, but rumors of spirits wandering the west bluff continued until the next century.

St. Francis Hospital

In 1832, the village of Peoria was a small frontier settlement with about 15 log cabins and only 2 wood frame houses. By 1845, Peoria had incorporated as a city and had a population of over 1,600.

In the 1840s in Peoria, there was little development of the downtown area. Drinking water came from public wells within the city. Sewers were open drains, and dirty water and sewage often mingled freely in the gutters. Sanitary facilities, when they existed at all, were of the crudest sort imaginable. In 1849, Peoria community leaders created a board of health to manage and prevent infectious disease. Infection was often spread by the open sewers and the dirty cesspools of water sitting in ditches within the city. The first pesthouse was established in the county courthouse and was then relocated near the city hospital in 1856. Peoria physicians at that time were largely private physicians, calling upon their wealthy patrons in the privacy and security of their own homes. The city hospital was inadequate for the growing population and provided only the most basic care.

The Peoria House of Corrections, or workhouse, was opened in 1879 at the foot of Grant Street adjacent to the river. The Isolation Hospital was formerly a part of the early workhouse. The workhouse closed in 1906, but part of the building continued to be used for the Isolation Hospital. The hospital could accommodate 60 patients and had three private rooms. It is rumored there was a cemetery on the grounds of the six acres of land that were used by the pesthouse, but the bodies were never recovered.

In 1875, a group of 16 Catholic nuns, led by Mother Mary Xavier, settled in Iowa City, Iowa. In order to obtain resources to serve the poor in the area, the sisters established collection groups that traveled into bordering states to generate money for their mission. One of these groups stopped in Peoria. In addition to Sr. Mary Frances Krasse (mother superior), there were five sisters: M. Barbara Markford, M. Liboria Pomberg, M. Thecla Mersch, M. Ositha Klostermann, and M. Theresia Garizen. Once in Peoria, they met with Fr. Bernard Baak, pastor of St. Thomas's church on the south side of Peoria. Working with Father Baak, the sisters went from door to door, caring for the sick and soliciting donations.

Recognizing the growing need in the community, Father Baak asked the sisters to start a hospital in the area. After receiving permission from Mother Superior Xavier in Iowa City, the six sisters moved to Peoria in October 1876 and rented a home at 708 South Adams Street. The new hospital was a two-story building that had a parlor on the main floor, operating room on the second floor, and five patient rooms. The sisters slept in the small quarters in the attic. There was a barn in the backyard that was used as an emergency chapel, and a small shack next door was used as a morgue.

The sisters provided a place of healing for the sick at no charge. They continued to work with Father Baak in providing for those in need in the area. Funding was limited, and the sisters endured many hardships. Rising at 5:00 a.m., the sisters began their day with morning mass before spending 8 to 10 hours in their services to the sick. They had no outside assistance and provided both hospital care and funeral services to the poor, sick, and needy.

In the spring of 1877, Peoria's first Catholic bishop of the Peoria diocese, John L. Spaulding, came to Peoria and visited the sisters at their hospital. He suggested the sisters start a new order and contacted Mother Mary Xavier back in Iowa City, requesting the sisters join with him in forming a religious community. On July 16, 1877, 10 sisters gathered and along with Bishop Spalding began the Sisters of the Third Order of St. Francis, Peoria, Illinois. Their mission was to follow the rule of St. Francis of Assisi to care for the ill and impoverished. The sisters elected Sr. Mary Frances Krasse as general mother of the order and sought a new building for their growing hospital.

The sisters acquired the old Underhill estate at 248 Northeast Glen Oak Avenue (then Bluff Street), owned by Lydia Moss Bradley in 1877. A three-story hospital was established at the site of the elaborate mansion at a cost of $10,500. The hospital quickly expanded to include accommodations for 54 patients. This imposing structure on the east bluff commanded an excellent view of downtown Peoria and the Illinois River. The sisters kept the bodies of deceased patients stored in a shed in the backyard until money could be raised for a burial. These patients paid 75¢ per day for hospitalization. The sisters supplemented the meager income by collecting donations door-to-door. They planted a garden on the hospital grounds and raised their own chickens and pigs.

When the hospital opened, there were 3 physicians in attendance and 19 sisters acting as nurses. Most of the hospital staff spoke German until 1927, when a decree was entered requiring all prayers to be conducted in English rather than German. When the hospital opened, beds on the main wards cost $4 to $6 per week; while those with more income and desiring a higher degree of privacy and comfort could rent private rooms from $7 to $10 per week. Not all of those staying at the hospital were ill; a large portion were mothers and children who were taken in

Mother Mary Frances Krasse is seen in 1885. (Courtesy of the Peoria Public Library.)

St. Francis Hospital stood at 248 Bluff Street and was partly razed in 1940. (Courtesy of the Peoria Public Library, Oakford Collection.)

Here is St. Francis Hospital as seen in 1918 and today. (Above, courtesy of the Peoria Public Library, Oakford Collection.)

as boarders. In its first year of operation, approximately one third of the hospital patients were charity patients, and nearly one third of those at the hospital were from other cities and towns.

Although originally called Bradley Hospital after Lydia Moss Bradley, the sisters executed a quitclaim deed that allowed them to change the name to the Sisters of the Third Order of St. Francis of the City of Peoria and County of Peoria. St. Francis Hospital was incorporated in 1880 and quickly expanded. Local physicians stepped forward to offer their services to the fledgling institution. The sisters prided themselves on the degree of devoted care and the cleanliness of their treatment areas, and they soon had hundreds of patients per year. The sisters lived from scraps of food collected from the community and provided every service to the patients, including transportation, housecleaning, maintenance, gardening, and washing the hospital laundry by hand.

The sisters firmly believed that a divine hand was guiding their work. There is a story of a contagious disease outbreak in 1885, with the sisters working themselves from sunrise into the early hours of the night, facing exhaustion and with little assistance from outside the hospital. Desperate, the sisters sent a messenger to go to the local physicians to enlist their aid. Shortly thereafter, three women dressed in white arrived to relieve the sisters of their work. Grateful and exhausted, the sisters let the three women take over and care for the sick. By morning, the sisters were well rested and looked for the women who had allowed them to refresh themselves. The women were nowhere to be found. Later that day, the messenger came back with word that no one in the community was able to come and help the sisters. The sisters realized the woman in white had not come from the community and that their prayers for assistance had been answered by a higher power. This is just one of the many examples of the miracles that have occurred at St. Francis over the years.

The 18-bed north wing of St. Francis was constructed in 1885, and Mother Krasse's dearest wish of a new chapel was realized. She developed tuberculosis and died on October 25, 1885, shortly after viewing the newly built chapel and sanctuary. She had been superior of St. Francis Hospital for nine years and had overseen a time of spiritual devotion and intense manual labor. She was also instrumental in starting new hospitals in Bloomington, Illinois; Burlington, Iowa; and Escanaba, Michigan. It is rumored that the spirit of Mother Krasse has never left the hospital grounds and remains to provide the same devoted care she gave so freely in life.

Following the death of Mother Krasse, St. Francis continued to expand. "Modern" operating rooms were added to the hospital in 1903, and there were over 250 operations performed per year in the early 1920s. Although crude by today's standards, the equipment at the time was considered state of the art. The 1901 original center building was destroyed in 1966 to make room for modernization in glass and steel. Construction and additions to St. Francis have been continuous over the years. Formal nurse training did not begin until 1905 and consisted mainly of bedside teaching by doctors and trained nurses as well as study from the few nursing books available at that time. The nursing school was accredited in 1914, and the first lay student started in 1918. The nursing school prerequisites were young women ages 19–30, with one year of high school, good hygiene, and good teeth. In 1936, a seven-story building was constructed for use as a nursing school, accommodating 250 student nurses.

The hospital bed capacity rose to 500 in 1942, and another building was constructed to add to the hospital complex. There were periodic polio epidemics from 1945 to 1955, affecting mainly children. A children's hospital was completed in 1954, and substantial additions were made to the existing structures in both 1963 and 1972. In 1974, the official name of the hospital was changed to St. Francis Hospital-Medical Center.

In 1982, St. Francis Hospital became St. Francis Medical Center. Today St. Francis Medical Center is one of the largest medical communities in downstate Illinois, with a staff of more than 4,000 employees and over 600 physicians. It is also one of the sites of reported ghostly sightings.

The Ghosts of St. Francis

The mission of St. Francis, to care for the ill and impoverished, has not changed since the inception of the institution in 1877. There are stories that many who assisted in this care have never abandoned their earthly mission and remain at the hospital to this day. These specters are a protective presence and watch out for both the staff and patients.

There are a number of ghosts that are reported to roam the halls of St. Francis. Nurses on the verge of falling asleep often report a soft tap on the arm or shoulder, waking them back to their duties. Upon regaining wakefulness, they report being alone in the area. The sound of rapid footsteps is often reported sounding through empty corridors.

The most prevalent reports are apparitions of nuns. One young woman recounted that she was finishing her night shift at the hospital and going through the walkway connecting the hospital to the parking area. She had reached midway along the corridor when she saw a nun approaching. The nun was dressed in very traditional garb, with the three-cornered hat and habit that were worn in the early 19th century. The young woman was very impressed by the elegance and old-fashioned appeal of her attire and was going to compliment the woman, but as she approached, the nun completely disappeared. She was in the corridor alone. She hastened out to her car, casting glances over her shoulder to see if the nun would follow. The woman is not alone; there have been many reports at the hospital of patients and workers who see nuns dressed in early-20th-century habits, gliding down the corridors or in and out of patient rooms.

In addition to the ghostly apparitions of nuns, there are also reports of patients who died in the hospital but continue to linger in the rooms. One former employee related that she worked as a nurse in the evenings in the late 1970s and early 1980s in one of the old wards. When she arrived for the night shift, the nurses were gathered around the nurses' station at the end of the hall. When she inquired as to the cause for alarm, she was informed that there was no patient in room 812 but that the emergency call light for the bathroom had lit at the nurses station. The group of nurses walked down to the room and discovered the bathroom door was locked. A strip of light shined through at the bottom of the door, so the nurses assumed a patient had wandered into the bathroom by mistake. This belief was strengthened when the nurses heard the unmistakable sound of someone being violently ill and vomiting in the toilet. The nurses banged on the door and inquired if the patient was okay and implored whoever was within to open the door. There was no response, so the nurses summoned the security guard. They stood watch outside the door waiting for security. Security soon arrived, and the nurses told them what they had seen and heard. The security officers used a master key to open the bathroom door. The group crowded around as the door swung open to reveal an empty room! There was no patient and nothing in the bathroom was disturbed. The nurses looked at one another and slowly made their way back to the nurses' station, discussing what they had experienced. The bathroom door was the only way into and out of the room, and there was no way someone could have climbed out the window as the room was on the eighth floor. Yet another mysterious encounter was attributed to the ghosts of St. Francis.

On another occasion, a nurse aide and charge nurse were walking down the hall in the same area of the hospital, discussing the evening work. They paused for a moment and were alarmed to hear the sound of their names whispered from a darkened room. They looked inside and determined there was no one there. Convinced they had been mistaken, they continued down the hall. Soon they again heard the whisper of their names, this time from both sides of the hall coming from the empty patient rooms. The nurses decided to cut short their walk and hustled back to the security of the nurses' station.

Another episode involved a nurse who was temporarily alone at the nurses' station. At the end of the hall, a patient call light came on for room 805. The nurse left the station and hurried down to the room. As she approached the bed, she noticed the patient lying there had a terrified expression on her face. She hurried over to the bed and leaned over the woman, asking what was wrong. The woman pulled her down toward the bed, clutching at her arm. "There is a ghost behind you," she whispered urgently. Startled, the nurse whirled around and looked behind her. There was no one there. She turned back to the woman and asked what she had seen. The patient brokenly told her that the image of a nun had appeared behind the nurse as she entered the room and had stood and watched them as they talked. The nurse moved the woman to a different room and closed the door to room 805.

Still another account of a supernatural encounter involved the neurological unit. Nurses conducted patient rounds at midnight, 2:00 a.m., 4:00 a.m. and 6:00 a.m. At that time, old cervical beds were used for patients who broke their necks. These beds consisted of a circular loop of metal, with the patient suspended inside the loop. In this way, the nurses were able to completely flip the patient either faceup or facedown to relieve pressure on the back. The cervical beds were large and cumbersome and required some strength to reposition the patient or move the bed. The beds were placed in the corner of a three-bed ward. On this particular night, a patient was receiving treatment for a broken neck. She was placed in the cervical bed and put in the corner of a room along with two other patients who were both comatose. When the nurses made the rounds at midnight, everything was in place and the woman in the cervical bed was repositioned. The nurses then left the room to continue their rounds. When they returned at 2:00 a.m., the nurses were astonished to discover the cervical bed had been pulled from the corner of the room and moved all the way across the floor, so the bed was blocking the door. The nurses woke up the patient and asked her what had happened to her bed. The patient was bewildered and related that she had been sound asleep, and when she woke her bed had been moved to the door. The nurses returned the bed to its original spot in the corner and made sure they traveled in pairs for the remainder of the evening.

The final story of ghostly encounters is an anecdote from a nurse who was also working the night shift. The nurse received a patient call to a room and went to answer the request. Upon arriving, the nurse noticed the patient was sound asleep. She woke her up and asked how she could help. The woman looked confused and said, "Oh, that's okay, the nun was already here and she helped me." The nurse was startled and asked the patient what had happened. The patient related that as soon as she had pressed the nurse call button, a nun in a long, black habit had appeared. She asked the nun to please help her reach the pitcher of water that was just out of reach on the table next to the bed. The nun had moved the table over so the water was accessible and then had left the room. The woman drank some water and dozed off just as the nurse arrived.

These are just some of the many stories surrounding St. Francis Hospital. If there is an entity or entities present, these are distinctly benevolent presences and, like the rest of the staff, only interested in patient welfare. St. Francis Medical Center remains one of the largest and busiest medical care centers in downstate Illinois, providing world-class healthcare to patients and employing a wide range of caring, dedicated professionals.

Nine

SINNERS

*Prohibition goes beyond the bounds of reason in that it attempts
to control a man's appetite by legislation and makes crimes out of things
that are not crimes. A prohibition law strikes a blow at the very
principles upon which our government was founded.*

—Abraham Lincoln

The Shelton Gang: America's Bloodiest Gang

Carl, Bernie, and Earl Shelton were born into a poor family of tenant farmers in southern Illinois in the early 1900s. They were three of eight children. Their parents were diligent, God-fearing people and labored to make ends meet for the family, while eking out a living on unproductive tracts of land around their home in Merriam. Eventually the couple acquired a 22-acre tract of their own. But times remained hard, and there was little money for anything but the bare necessities.

From an early age, the three Shelton boys displayed an aversion to the farmwork that enslaved their parents and other siblings. They obtained a marginal education but were able to read and write. The trio acquired enough street smarts and personal charisma to carry them out of the southern Illinois dirt. During their formative years, the group began their criminal career, taking part in petty thievery and destruction of property, crimes that would eventually evolve into felony burglary and robbery.

The Shelton boys moved to East St. Louis in 1917 and opened a saloon. East St. Louis at that time was a rough blue-collar town, consisting mainly of factory workers and miners. Daily alcohol consumption was a way of life for the men in the area, as they emerged exhausted and grimy from the mines and sought comfort at the local watering hole. The Shelton saloon prospered under these circumstances, and the Shelton boys were able to afford the clothing and cars that displayed their newly acquired wealth. But change was on its way in the form of Prohibition, and although it would end their legitimate business, it would open up new paths of revenue.

Prohibition began in 1919, and it quickly proved a golden opportunity for many Illinois criminals to satiate the still-thirsty crowd and strike it rich in the process. While many citizens publicly supported Prohibition, there proved to be a large number of Americans willing to become first-time criminals by making their own bathtub gin or paying top dollar for bootleg liquor. Thus began a national market with distribution and sales in every state. Jazz, flappers, and speakeasies became the rage, and petty thugs quickly found they could become industry giants in this illicit world.

The Shelton boys had to close down their saloon but found a new and highly profitable enterprise in bootlegging. Although a number of gangsters emerged on the scene, eager to take over the southern Illinois territory, the Shelton brothers quickly grew in renown due to a rapport with the local workers and contacts in the area. Carl Shelton became the leader of the gang, with Earl and Bernie distributing illegal alcohol and bribing local officials to turn a blind eye to their operations. Carl and Earl were adept at smooth-talking their way into the good graces of police and politicians. They had an easy affinity with authority figures; Carl was dapper and distinguished, while Earl was affable and friendly. But if Carl and Earl were the brains, that left Bernie to be the brawn. Bernie was surly, tough, and had a reputation as a mean drunk with a quick temper. If Carl and Earl could not persuade local shop owners that they needed to run their operations through the Shelton gang, Bernie would go in and persuade them by less gentle means.

The Birger-Shelton War and the Kincaid Robbery

During Prohibition, two gangs emerged in central southern Illinois, the Shelton gang, run by Carl Shelton, and the Birger Gang, headed by Charles Birger. However, the gangs were united against an even bigger threat in southern Illinois at that time, the Ku Klux Klan. The Klan members advocated "pure Americanism," and in the 1920s its focus was on those individuals and organizations that defied Prohibition. The early 1920s was a bloody time in southern Illinois, with a public desensitized to violence by the death of 21 people in a Herrin mine strike in 1922 and at least a dozen murders by the Ku Klux Klan between 1924 and 1925.

For a short time, the gangs united against their common foe, and the Birger-Shelton Gang became very wealthy with the combined industry in stolen car sales, bootleg liquor, and roadhouses. However, the camaraderie proved short-lived. As the Klan lost power in southern Illinois, the Birger and Shelton Gangs each realized the profitably of eliminating the competition. The final break in the partnership came when William Holland, a bodyguard for Carl Shelton, was gunned down by Birger henchmen outside a roadhouse in Herrin.

The Birger and Shelton Gangs took the war to the streets and engaged in open battle for control of the southern Illinois region. Both sides fashioned "war wagons" from cars plated with armor and engaged in tactics such as drive-by shootings and ambush attacks. The violence quickly escalated, and there followed a coordinated airplane attack in the first-ever American civilian bombing. When open warfare failed to establish either as the victor, the gangs decided to take their vendetta to a new venue and moved the battle into federal court. Charlie Birger accused the Shelton Gang of robbing a mail car in Collinsville. Carl, Earl, and Bernie were all incarcerated temporarily. They obtained their release after it was proven that at least one witness had perjured himself in giving court testimony against the Sheltons. Their freedom would prove short-lived.

On September 27, 1924, Carl, Earl, and Bernie Shelton, along with three other men, loaded their guns and walked into a bank in Kincaid. They approached the teller's window and, brandishing weapons, demanded that everyone in the bank drop to the ground. The group was surprised when, instead of meek compliance, one of the bank workers opened fire and pushed the burglar alarm. The gang fired back, and in the crossfire one of the cashiers ran for the vault. The robbers followed and ordered the cashier to get into the vault and open the safe. The cashier explained that the safe could not be opened due to a time lock, and the thwarted and infuriated gang stuffed $7,785 of counter money into a satchel and ran for the door. By this time the local citizenry, alerted by the sound of gunfire from the bank, had organized a group of gunmen and were waiting for the robbers. The street resonated with the sound of bullets as the gang attempted to escape. In their efforts to get past the vigilantes, the robbers took the cashier along with them as a hostage and hustled him toward a Cadillac that was parked near the bank. The gunmen made a run for the car as the bullets rained down on every side. The robber holding the satchel of cash was shot in the leg by a local citizen and dropped the satchel. There was no time to recover the money. Using a sawed off shotgun, the robbers made their escape. The cashier was released uninjured in a field on their way out of town. Miraculously, no one was fatally injured in the gunfight.

The Shelton boys emerged with nothing to show for their efforts except bullet wounds and a black eye to their local reputation. They continued their management of roadhouses and

Here is notorious gangster Bernie Shelton. (Courtesy of the Peoria Journal Star *Archives.)*

Seen here is Earl Shelton. (Courtesy of the Peoria Journal Star *Archives.)*

management of bootleg operations. Although the local wheels of justice turned slowly, they did turn, and a grand jury indictment came down three years later on August 29, 1927. The indictment named the Shelton boys and their three accomplices in the Kincaid robbery. The trial was a media circus, with long lines of spectators waiting for hours outside the courthouse to catch a glimpse of the infamous Shelton boys. The courthouse was packed to maximum capacity with gang members, spectators, and press. The trial commenced with a group of eyewitnesses presented by the prosecution who could tie the Shelton brothers to the scene of the crime. The witness testimony was uncorroborated and, for the most part, unconvincing. Still the defense had an uphill battle, and in a surprising twist, Bernie and Earl were assisted by an unlikely ally that caused a public sensation. Detective Sergeant O'Rourke of the East St. Louis police department appeared and testified that Bernie and Earl Shelton were both incarcerated in the East St. Louis police station at the time of the robbery. To prove this claim, a police blotter was introduced into evidence that clearly showed the names of Bernie and Earl Shelton and the dates and times of their incarceration. These dates coincided with the Kincaid bank robbery. The prosecution cried foul and pointed out that the police blotter had clearly been subject to tampering, with all other names on the same date in faded ink, and the Shelton boys' names standing out boldly in fresh, blue ink. Nonetheless, the defense stood by the alibi provided by the police department, which unfortunately did not account for the whereabouts of Carl Shelton.

Carl sought to prove he had been in East St. Louis the entire day of the robbery by introducing witnesses, including a taxicab driver and car salesmen who claimed to have seen him and the other Shelton boys in town at various times. Despite the defense evidence, the jury deliberated only five hours before returning a verdict of guilty against the three Shelton brothers. Each was sentenced to one year of incarceration at Chester.

The defense quickly sought a new trial, introducing affidavits from a number of eyewitnesses that reported that their testimony at trial had been coerced and/or was false. The Shelton gang claimed they were victims of a frame-up, and the case proceeded all the way to the Illinois Supreme Court. The court found that the defense had not had time to prepare to cross-examine the witnesses who had not been produced prior to trial and further found the eyewitness testimony placing the Shelton brothers at the scene was not convincing. The court remanded the case back to the lower court for a new trial. The case languished for a few years, and eventually the new state's attorney elected not to retry. The Shelton brothers were free again, and those involved in the Kincaid bank robbery were never brought to justice.

The Shelton gang wasted no time in resuming its bootleg activities and quickly became the biggest liquor wholesalers in downstate Illinois. They also expanded their gambling ties and talked their way into slot machine markets all over downstate Illinois. The Sheltons were earning millions of dollars at a time when the rest of the country was sunk in the Great Depression. The Birger-Shelton war continued but was inflicting heavy casualties for both sides. By 1926, the gang conflict had resulted in a total of 16 members dead. Charlie Birger's control of his gang had weakened with the release of the Shelton boys from prison, and the hired guns in the lower ranks of the Birger gang sought to take advantage of Charlie's loss of power by testifying against their former boss in exchange for prosecutorial immunity. Charlie was eventually convicted of ordering the execution of West City mayor Joe Adams and sentenced to death for first-degree murder. Charlie appealed the sentence and attempted an insanity plea, but the court rejected this argument. Charlie was publicly hanged on April 19, 1928, for his crimes.

By the 1930s, the final members of the Birger gang had been incarcerated; and the Shelton brothers were free to expand their operation far into south and central Illinois with virtually no competition from other groups. The federal government had been investigating the Shelton operations for many years and charged Carl and Earl with violation of the Prohibition laws.

However, the Shelton brothers successfully evaded any criminal convictions and were able to turn their undivided attention to the creation of a gambling empire.

It was becoming clear to the nation that Prohibition had failed. In 1933, Congress passed the 21st Amendment, which repealed the 18th Amendment and ended Prohibition. Local governments in Illinois were irked by the Shelton gang's unchecked power, as well as its success in evading incarceration. The Downstate Crime Commission was established to end the Shelton gang by whatever means necessary. The rogue commission ambushed and arrested most members of the gang. Sensing danger, the Shelton boys quietly withdrew from the public eye, retiring to their respective farms to run small gambling establishments. Despite the appearance that the Shelton brothers were no longer actively involved in the gangster business, Carl, Earl, and Bernie kept a hand in most of the rackets in the state by acting as partners to local gamblers. This included a gambling partnership with Clyde Garrison in Peoria.

The Shelton Gang in Peoria

Clyde Garrison controlled gambling in Peoria in the 1930s but was troubled by the threat of violence from Chicago mobsters. The Chicago operatives had become increasingly restless as they saw wasted opportunities for easy revenue in central and southern Illinois. After the Shelton brothers went into semiretirement, the Chicago mobsters became bolder in their efforts to branch out. Many of these gangsters targeted Clyde Garrison and the Peoria market. Garrison and his wife were attacked in a drive-by shooting, and his wife died in a barrage of machine gun fire. Garrison was badly shaken and invited Carl Shelton into a partnership for control of gambling operations in Peoria. The Sheltons provided Garrison much-needed protection from the Chicago groups, who saw the Shelton Gang as a viable threat in the area. Garrison eventually retired and left the Peoria game wide-open to the Shelton brothers.

In the early 1900s, Peoria had a rough-and-tumble reputation as a lawless frontier town that had earned it the nickname "Roaring Peoria." It was also a town of great prosperity and industry, with whiskey distilleries pouring out booze and manufacturers flooding the marked with every product that might appeal to midwestern taste and sensibility. Peoria was a prominent stop on the vaudeville tour, and was also known for its open policy regarding liquor and prostitution. Its abundance of corn for production of grain alcohol and situation on the Illinois River made Peoria one of the largest manufacturers of whiskey in the United States.

When the Shelton Gang came to town, gamblers and prostitutes rubbed elbows with politicians and public officials. The shanties, slums, brothels, and wagering houses along the Peoria riverfront stood in sharp contrast to the elaborate and elegant mansions built high along the bluffs on High Street and Moss Avenue. Peoria was working hard to earn its title of "Saturday Night City," providing both locals and tourists with access to every imaginable vice. Visitors would frequently mention the town's distinctive odor, a blend of hops and yeast from the whiskey distilleries and breweries operating all over town. The town was a gambler's paradise, with cheap liquor, easy women, and little interference from local government in pursuit of these vices.

The mayor of Peoria at the time, Edward Woodruff, turned a blind eye to most of the disreputable enterprises in town and used the greed of the underbelly for the public coffer. A crap table would cost a $500 kickback to the city, a roulette wheel $250. Mayor Woodruff used the revenue generated to build bridges, repair streets, and fund city projects.

With the silent approval of Mayor Woodruff, the Sheltons enjoyed a period of unprecedented peace and prosperity in Peoria in the early 1940s. Carl was unofficially appointed to take charge of making the payoffs necessary to keep the local gaming operations running, and public officials turned a blind eye in exchange for a piece of the pie. For the first time, Carl was able to keep his hands clean by calling on Bernie to do the dirty work and in the process achieved a modicum of social acceptance. Carl bought a house at 1308 North Knoxville Avenue in Peoria in 1943 and by all accounts was a model neighbor and citizen.

Carl brought in brothers Bernie and Earl to assist in running his gaming establishments. One of their primary responsibilities was to convince other businessmen in the community that it was in their best interest to partner with the Shelton Gang. The Sheltons bought the Palace Club, a bar and gambling establishment in the 200 block of South Madison Street, directly across from city hall. From their headquarters, the Shelton Gang was at the center of downtown Peoria and the hub of gambling activity in the city. There were rumors the gang uncovered and utilized underground tunnels that had been established in the early days of the village of New Peoria. There were also stories that the huge underground wine vaults that had been built in the late 1700s were used by the Shelton Gang to store firearms and hold meetings.

The reign of prosperity came to an end with the mayoral election in 1945. The citizenry was fed up with Peoria's reputation for lawlessness and vice and elected Mayor Carl O. Triebel, owner of Ideal Troy cleaners. Triebel did not run under a reform ticket, but his name soon became synonymous with change, and that change would end the Shelton power. At that time, it was reported that many of Peoria's aldermen were receiving substantial monthly payments from the slot machine racket. Triebel quickly cracked down on illegal gambling in the city. He was straightforward in his approach to crime and personally informed Carl Shelton that he was shutting down the slot machines in Peoria, thus divesting Carl of much of his gambling revenue. Instead of engaging in warfare with the new mayor, Carl elected to semiretire to his farm in Fairfield and care for his dogs and horses.

Bernie Shelton was not so easily dissuaded in retiring his gangster status and found a niche in Peoria County. Bernie moved the Shelton headquarters from the Palace Club in downtown Peoria to the Parkside Tavern on Farmington Road. Farther out on Farmington Road, Bernie owned and operated Golden Rule Farm. Carl continued to live in Peoria at least part-time and provided an advisory role to Bernie. He was often reported seen conferring with Bernie and other members of the Shelton Gang down at the Parkside Tavern.

The Chicago mob recognized that with Carl no longer at the helm, the Shelton territory was potentially up for grabs. This belief was enforced when some of the Shelton Gang underlings joined forces with the Chicago element. It was common knowledge in the underworld that there was a price of $10,000 on the heads of both Carl and Bernie and that mobsters in both Chicago and St. Louis had formed an alliance to eliminate the Shelton Gang. There were a number of attempts to ambush the Sheltons in Peoria, but none were successful. Thugs with close ties to the Sheltons were increasingly coming under attack, and three associates were killed in a short period in 1946.

The End of the Shelton Gang

The Sheltons' reign came to a bloody end beginning with the murder of Carl Shelton in 1947. Carl had not settled peacefully in Fairfield and was often engage in violent arguments with neighbors over the theft of his prize cattle. As a result of this turmoil, Carl decided to sell his farm and left on the morning of October 23, 1947, to attend a business meeting with regard to the sale. Carl was traveling in a jeep alone, and closely following was a truck with Ray Walker, a close business associate, and Little Earl Shelton, nephew to Big Earl. The two vehicles approached a small bridge on Pond Creek Road, a short way from State Highway 15. As they approached the bridge, the men heard what was later described as a series of horns blaring, one long and two short honks. Once the men arrived at the bridge, they were ambushed by heavy and intense gunfire coming from dense brush on the other side. Carl fell out of the jeep and onto the gravel road. Ray Walker and Little Earl Shelton jumped uninjured from the truck and hid in the ditch under the bridge. The attacker's car, a black Ford sedan, was sitting on the other side of the road near the bridge, parked in underbrush. Ray Walker and Little Earl Shelton would later report that they overheard Carl begging for his life in the road over the bridge. His last words were supposedly, "Don't shoot me any more, Charlie. It's me, Carl Shelton. You've killed me already." The reply was more gunshots. Carl's body was found about a foot from the top of the ditch with his head and face facing downward toward the creek. Carl had 25 bullet holes in his body coming from at least 17 different kinds of bullets.

Carl's funeral was held in Fairfield and was the largest event of its kind in the history of the town. Following the funeral, the estate was inventoried for the purpose of dividing the assets. Carl's estate was surprisingly modest, and he had just under $10 in his local bank account at the time of his death. Rumors abounded regarding Carl's lost fortune, and speculation was rampant that the majority of his money had been hidden in a secret vault or safe in Peoria. No money from the estate was ever recovered.

The coroner's inquest led to a warrant for the arrest of Charlie Harris, identified by Ray Walker and Little Earl Shelton as one of the men fleeing from the scene of the attack. However, the grand jury returned no indictment against him, and Harris was a free man. The murderers of Carl Shelton would never be brought to justice.

Following Carl's death, other members of the Shelton gang began turning over their operations and territory to the Chicago–St. Louis alliance. However, Bernie Shelton still had aspirations to become the city boss and was not interested in sharing the Peoria operation with any outsiders. He repeatedly rebuffed attempts by the alliance to negotiate a truce to share the territory. Bernie continued the payoffs that Carl had overseen and began to establish himself as the head of the gambling activity in Peoria. However, Bernie's personal demons in the form of an explosive temperament, poor judgment, and excessive alcohol consumption led to a public brawl at the Parkside Tavern in 1948. A. L. Hunt, proprietor of a drive-in across Farmington Road from the tavern, was witness to the brawl, and Bernie was subsequently charged with felony assault. The state's attorney, Roy Hull, headed the grand jury investigation. However, justice would be denied in the traditional fashion since Bernie would die before he could stand trial.

On July 26, 1948, at 10:00 a.m., Bernie drove from his Golden Rule Farm to the Parkway Tavern. Once there, Bernie requested that Alex Ronitis, a bartender at the Parkway, follow him to the Buick dealership so he could get his car repaired. At approximately 10:45 a.m., the pair walked out of the Parkway Tavern and headed toward the parking lot. However, Ronitis claimed he had left his cigarettes inside and ducked back into the tavern. Bernie kept walking toward his car in the parking lot. He was nearly to the car when a shot rang out from the wooded area behind the tavern. The bullet struck Bernie near his heart and passed through his right side. Bernie fell across the hood and front bumper of his car, mortally wounded. Ronitis had been about to join Bernie, but when he heard the shot he stopped at the front door of the tavern. When he opened the door a few minutes later, he reported that he saw Bernie crouched by the front wheel of his car, and Ronitis claimed that as he began to move forward Bernie waved his arm, indicating that Ronitis should remain inside the tavern. Ronitis held the door open, and Bernie crawled through the gravel back into the Parkway. Bernie was assisted onto a barstool by Ronitis and another bartender and reported to Ronitis that someone had shot him from the woods. Bernie was bleeding heavily from a large chest wound, and Ronitis called for an ambulance. By the time the ambulance arrived, Bernie insisted he was not badly injured and refused a stretcher, walking himself out to the waiting vehicle. On the way to the hospital, Bernie thought his shooters were giving chase and cautioned the ambulance attendants to keep an eye on the car behind them. By the time the ambulance reached the hospital, Bernie realized he was mortally wounded and requested removal of his slacks and shoes. Bernie died at St. Francis Hospital at 11:46 a.m. at the age of 49.

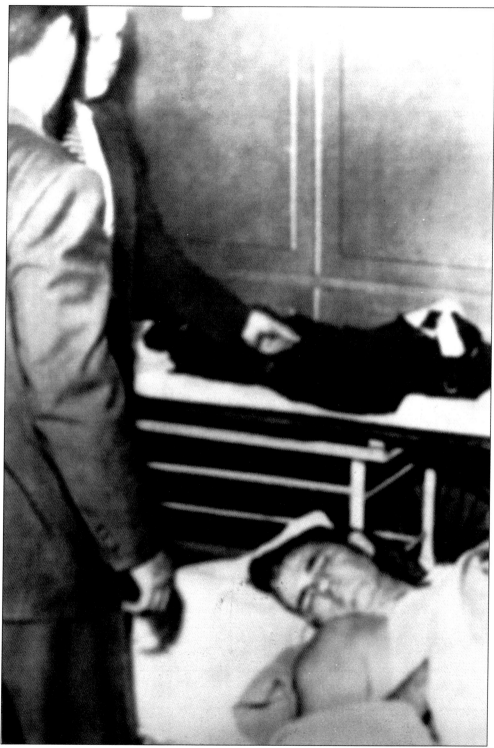

Bernie Shelton's body is seen at the morgue following his murder at the Parkway Inn. (Courtesy of the Peoria Journal Star Archives.)

Here is the former Parkway Inn. The door at right is where Bernie Shelton walked out and was gunned down. His spirit reportedly still haunts the building.

Chief Deputy Sheriff Bill Littell led a search of the woods behind Parkway Tavern and recovered cartridge shells and a .351 Winchester rifle from the underbrush. The killer or killers had apparently driven to St. Joseph's Cemetery and parked on the hill above the tavern. One shooter then walked down the slope and shot Bernie with the automatic rifle.

A search for the killers was made, but no one was ever arrested for the crime. The rifle was subject to fingerprint and ballistics testing, but this did not produce any evidence or leads. Investigators later learned that a dark green car, likely a Chevy Sedan, had entered St. Joseph cemetery around 10:30 that morning, and the sharply dressed driver and his companion had been seen by a few caretakers. They drove through the cemetery to park at the slope above Parkway Tavern. The two men were never identified. The death of Bernie Shelton was never solved, and investigators concluded he was the victim of a mob hit by gangsters in either Chicago or St. Louis.

Bernie's body was laid out in an expensive casket in the front room of his Golden Acre Farm in Peoria. Crowds lined up for a chance to view Bernie's body, and a long procession of expensive cars formed a funeral procession to Parkview cemetery. Like Carl, Bernie's estate failed to reveal the riches many had long-expected the brothers were hording. Bernie's personal estate was valued at $13,000, and as with Carl, speculation spread that Bernie had hidden the majority of his estate to avoid interference from the federal government. Rumors persist of secret underground rooms and tunnels in an intricate network in downtown Peoria that were used by the Shelton brothers and other gangsters in their illegal activities. There are also reports of a hidden vault in the tunnels where the Sheltons kept the majority of their illegal profits, the location long since lost to time.

The death of Bernie Shelton was the end of the infamous Shelton gang and the end of the era of the boss gangster in Peoria. Although there were racketeers in Chicago and southern Illinois eager to tap into the Peoria market, they never achieved the widespread success and acceptance enjoyed by the Shelton brothers. Journalists tapped into the market, exposing the years of official payoffs and corruption that had allowed the Shelton brothers to flourish. It was reported that state's attorney Roy Hull had sought to collect a $25,000 bribe from Bernie shortly before his murder, in exchange for dismissing the felony assault charge. Hull, along with other officials, was indicted, but that indictment was later dropped after investigation. Public outrage fed reform, and investigations were started in nearly every county in Illinois to examine a possible tie between the gangsters and public officials.

In 1952, Peoria's form of government changed from mayor-council to manager-council, thus limiting the amount of power held by the mayoral office. By 1953, Peoria was selected as one of the year's All-American Cities.

The era of the gangster was over. Big Earl Shelton was understandably reluctant to leave his farm in Fairfield and did not venture into Peoria. His precaution would not save him from the wages of sin, and he was gunned down on May 24, 1949, at the local Farmer's Club. Little Earl Shelton and Ray Walker were also targets of the type of gun violence they had so long perpetuated. No one was ever arrested for the murders or assaults on the Shelton family. In April 1951, the Sheltons sold almost all their land and holdings in Illinois, and the family fled to Florida. The once-mighty Shelton Gang retired into the stuff of local legend.

Shadows and Ghosts

Following the death of Bernie Shelton at the Parkside Tavern, the owners of that establishment began to report strange activity. It was said that Bernie Shelton never left the Parkside and manifests his presence by switching on and off the lights at random times and moving items on the bar. Bar patrons report feeling breathing on their necks or the feel of an icy hand on their back or arms. Other reports include the sound of gunshots near the parking lot and mysterious yellow headlights that appear above the bar in St. Joseph's Cemetery. Gusts of wind whip through the tavern and blow open the front door where Bernie had crawled for refuge. This occurs even on days when there is no noticeable breeze. During his life, Bernie Shelton sought desperately to retain control of Peoria at the Parkside, and many say he has never given up. His restless spirit wanders the tavern and parking lot, seeking to regain the power of the Shelton heyday in Roaring Peoria.

Ten

AROUND THE AREA

Man being immortal, to make him wise only for this world is
not worth the pains; but to make him wise unto eternal
life, is worthy of all efforts . . . This is the college's primary
objective, and without attain this it fails of its end.
—Philander Chase, on the dedication of Jubilee College, 1842

Jubilee College and State Park

In the early 1800s, there were 22 million acres of prairie in Illinois, most of it concentrated in the central region of the state. Wooded hills, broad meadows, and a variety of wildflowers and vegetation soaked in the sticky summer heat and braved the cold winds that mercilessly ripped across the prairie in the winter. Fifteen minutes northwest of Peoria lays Jubilee College and Jubilee State Park, encompassing over 3,000 acres in central Illinois. Jubilee Creek winds through the area, eventually joining Kickapoo Creek and the Illinois River. Although there are hiking and equestrian trails, the majority of the park remains a sprawling wilderness, ideal for intrepid hikers and weekend explorers. Most of these temporary visitors are unaware of the park's size and the vast population of wildlife in the area: coyote, fox, pheasant, raccoon, squirrel, beaver, muskrat, skunk, and white-tailed deer all make their homes here. The forests surrounding the area run into gentle sloping rises, with lush tall-grass prairie, and wildflowers growing in cheerful and ramshackle abandon.

Jubilee College sits majestically among the rolling hills and lacy leaves of great oak trees, quietly sleeping in the prairie air. Jubilee College was founded in 1839, the brainchild of Philander Chase, the first Episcopal bishop in Illinois. In the summer of 1835, Chase was appointed to the Episcopate of Illinois. Chase accepted the appointment and quickly made plans to establish a seminary in Illinois. Chase resolved to return to England, where he had raised some $30,000 to found a seminary in Ohio almost 20 years earlier, to generate funds for the construction of a new theological institution in the wild prairie land of Illinois. His efforts paid off, and he was rewarded with a large check from one of his noble patrons to be used for his work in Illinois.

Philander Chase was 60 years old when he came to Jubilee, which was at that time merely an outpost in the rugged and wild frontier of Illinois. He had a vision of establishing a sprawling theological institution in the west, a place to educate and influence young men and women and strengthen their faith. Chase came to Peoria on November 17, 1834, traveling by pony from Chicago to Peoria, a distance of 160 miles. He performed the first Episcopal services on November 19, 1834, noting that there was no school, no minister, and no organized society for any religious services. The only church in Peoria County at that time was St. Jude's Church. When Chase arrived, Peoria was a rough frontier town, with 70–80 houses and 400–500 inhabitants. A brick courthouse was in the process of being built, and few shops lined the main streets of downtown.

Chase quickly chose a site for his new school and constructed a crude log house, Robin's Nest, so called because it was built of mud and sticks and filled with children. Chase deliberately chose a spot in the country, where he could maintain strict control and where the students would not

This is the original construction of Jubilee College as it looked in 1841. (Courtesy of the Kenyon College Archives.)

be tempted by the sins of the city. By 1838, Chase had purchased 2,500 acres of land in Peoria County for the new college. He named the college Jubilee, in gratitude to God and rejoicing that he had come through his struggles at Ohio. A chapel and schoolroom were built on Jubilee Hill, one mile from Robin's Nest, in 1840–1841. A dormitory extended over the schoolroom, and a balcony overlooked the chapel. Laborers and teams of oxen hauled stone, sand, lime, and other building materials to the site. Jubilee College consisted of a theological department, college, preparatory school for boys, and finishing school for girls. Jubilee was one of the state's earliest educational institutions. The preparatory school generated the most revenue for the college, teaching students Greek, Latin, reading, writing, and mathematics. Fees for Jubilee started at $100 in 1840 for a term, and included books, room, board, and tuition. The fee eventually went up to $150 in 1855. Funding for the college came from England and from friends of Philander Chase in New Orleans and Charleston.

Laying of the cornerstone of Jubilee chapel took place on April 3, 1839. Philander Chase was in some respects rigid in his thinking and made quite a few enemies in the area by constantly chastising colleagues for what he saw as indifference or laziness. Many clergy would not have dreamed of embracing a life on the difficult Illinois frontier, and Chase was quite vocal in what he saw as a dereliction of Christian duty. Chase was also quite boastful regarding his own accomplishments and very demanding with those he felt were in a position to help him financially and in his view had a moral obligation to do so.

Jubilee was not just a theological institution; it was a community in itself. Farming, sharecropping, and livestock helped to bring in much-needed revenue. There was also a sawmill, grain mill, and print shop. At a time when clergymen were discouraged from taking on any work that could be considered menial or physically laborious under church rules, Philander Chase found life on the frontier presented a new reality, and he routinely engaged in duties such as cutting and hauling wood, caring for livestock, and building fires. The frontier was a great equalizer, and Philander Chase acknowledged that he had undertaken tasks undreamed of by his fellow brethren in the east. Chase had long-embraced adventure and hardship in pursuit of his religious vision. He was a large man, in both vision and size, and wore his velvet skullcap and cassock coat with authority around the grounds.

At the time he was attempting to establish Jubilee, Chase was having his share of personal trials and heartache. His son George was wild and immoral, and for a man of Chase's integrity, his deficiencies in character were especially painful. Chase was often seen walking the grounds, letter in hand, shaken by the latest news of his son's indiscretions. His grief was especially evident in his personal correspondence.

PRIVATE DATED March 25, 1822
Brother Dudley then shewed me a letter from his wife about George: Dreadful to relate-he is returned to all his former drunken habits!! Eliza his wife says that he has been in the habit of taking opium ever since he came back from N. York!!!-O my poor heart! I have no hope but in God's miraculous grace to change the heart of this my *** son. Let us cry for this, day and night, and cease not till God have mercy on us!- O father of mercies! Visit not my sins on the head of this wretched son! For Jesus sake, pity and convert him before he go home with all his sins about him!- Do Dear Wife with me, his unhappy father, pray for this my wretched son. Strive earnestly for Jesus' sake that God would have mercy on him.

New York June 6, 1828 Half past nine P.M.
My dear wife:
If you know all my sorrows and griefs and mortifications and disappointments it would make you pity more than ever. ***** I have written long letters to Brother Dudley about George.

What can be done I know not. He will he has determined to die a vagabond a vagrant. He thinks he can in this way make his friends feel his consequence of sin and no other way. I have gotten my dispatches ready for England (and they are very voluminous almost) they go the day after tomorrow. Do love your most distractful but most faithful and loving husband.

If his personal tragedies were not enough, Chase's professional life was also facing challenges. Although Jubilee College flourished initially, by the early 1840s, a series of disasters struck the small school. Hoof-and-mouth disease decimated the population of farm animals. The Kickapoo River flooded and drowned the crops, thereby denying the school of most of its revenue for the year. The grain mill burned to the ground. To cover expenses, Chase sold much of the college land, decreasing the size of the endowment. At the same time Jubilee was facing these crises, neighboring educational institutions opened, competing for the few students of higher learning at that time.

At the end of his life, Philander Chase was keenly aware that his vision had failed to come to fruition and that Jubilee had not achieved the greatness that he had hoped for when he first embraced the rough Illinois frontier. Chase was a man of grand ideas and passion for theological advancement and had foreseen an institution on par with those colleges established by his illustrious colleagues in the east. He struggled on until the end of his life but must have realized he was facing an uphill and thankless battle.

The final loss to Jubilee College was the death of Philander Chase in 1852. Bishop Chase had been out driving with his wife when an accident caused the horses to bolt, pulling him from the carriage. Bishop Chase never recovered from his injuries and died in his room at Jubilee. His body was buried on the grounds in the Jubilee churchyard.

Following the death of Bishop Chase, the situation grew grim for Jubilee. In 1857, the west wing dormitory of the college was destroyed by fire. The year 1860 brought about the opening volley of the Civil War, and funds previously coming from Chase's connections in New Orleans and Charleston were redirected to the war effort. Jubilee College finally closed its doors in 1862.

After years of decay and abandonment, the college was placed for auction in 1933. It was purchased by Dr. George Zeller. Dr. Zeller donated the 93 acres left from Chase's endowment to the Boy Scouts of America and the college building to the Episcopal Church of Peoria.

The original college building and Strawberry College still stand, along with the churchyard. Outside the park, Chase's residence, Robin's Nest, also remains. The Jubilee churchyard, God's Acre, lies west of the college, to the north side of the main road through Jubilee Park. A white marble monument to Philander Chase commemorates his birth and contributions to the state.

Despite Bishop Chase's conviction as to the rightness of his venture, he suffered from frequent bouts of depression over what he perceived was the lack of support among his brethren and his personal grief over his son. The letters of Bishop Chase frequently mention his melancholy and deep dejection over the scarce resources provided the parish and the limited manpower for such a large venture.

Bishop Chase's life reminisces sadly ended with a question: "Will the writer's friends see him sink into his grave and be buried on Jubilee hill without the completion of his great design, for which he has, to this late period of his life be laboring?"

Ghosts of Jubilee

Many visiting Jubilee College are struck by the austerity and sadness that seem to hang in the air here, as though the personal and professional disappointments of Philander Chase have permeated the stone of the college itself. There are many reports of mysterious cold spots throughout the college. There are also reports of strange lights at night, giving the appearance

The former dormitory is the oldest section of Jubilee College. Lights can often be seen passing by the windows at night.

God's Acre Cemetery is the final resting place of Bishop Philander Chase.

Bishop Chase

Æ 77

Chase's spirit is said to still haunt the grounds of Jubilee College.

of flickering candlelight passing by the windows of Chase Hall, the former dormitory. Mysterious footsteps have also been reported by those touring the site, the sound of heels striking the floor cross the upper attic in a restless pace, back and forth.

One visitor recounted how she and her family were taking a tour of the college and were walking through the former chapel when she detected a movement out of the corner of her eye. After she left the college, she told her family that she had seen a man standing in front of one of the chapel windows, staring sightlessly onto the park grounds. He was very tall and dressed in a dark robe with a tight cap on his head. She saw him one instant, and in the next moment he was gone. At the same time, there was a rush of cold air through the chapel, which her companions commented on at the time, even though they had not seen the figure. Although her companions wanted to return to the college, she felt as though she had had enough exposure to the dark side of Jubilee.

Other visitors have similarly reported the sight of an older man, wearing a long dark robe and small cap, walking past the upper-story windows of the former dormitory. There are also tales of strange mists arising in the area around Philander Chase's grave and then dispersing in pure sunlight.

In addition to the stories regarding Bishop Chase, there is also the legend of "Maiden Leap." The story goes that there was a young and beautiful Native American maiden whose tribe lived in the area that is now Jubilee State Park. The young maiden had two rivals for her affections. She could not decide which young buck she preferred and finally told them she had devised a test that would decide her future mate. She told the two that there was a spot chosen over a cliff, and when she gave the signal, they should both run and throw themselves over the precipice. The one that did not die would win her hand in marriage. The young men were understandably reluctant to undertake this course of action, but finally one dared the other to try it. The bucks agreed, and they both lined up at the spot chosen by the young maiden. At her signal, they took off at a full run toward the edge of the cliff, but just before they got to the precipice one stopped suddenly and the other plunged to his death on the rocks below. The maiden honored her promise and married the buck who did not jump. There are reports that the sound of the young buck's war cry as he leapt from the cliff still reverberates through the park.

Jubilee College State Historic Site has expanded from its original 93 acres to more than 3,200 and became Jubilee College State Park. Jubilee College was added to the National Register of Historic Places in 1972. The site was briefly closed by former governor Rod Blagojevich on November 30, 2008. Like so many of the historical sites in and around the Peoria area, Jubilee may not be accessible for future generations without more public interest and involvement.

Grandview Drive

In 1881, Lydia Moss Bradley bequeathed a tract of land to the City of Peoria for use as a park. The City Beautiful movement was popular in the country in the early 20th century as a response to increasing industrialism, pollution, and urban congestion. In Peoria, progressive city officials were eager to create a scenic drive and park in the heart of the city. The Pleasure Driveway and Park District of Peoria was established on March 15, 1894. The district purchased tracts of land throughout the city to create parks and recreational areas. A scenic roadway was proposed for Prospect Drive, with a view of the Illinois River and rolling bluffs below. Landscape gardener and architect Oscar Dubuis was employed by the Peoria Park District to develop the land and construct the parkway. Dubuis also designed Glen Oak Park, Laura Bradley Park, and Trewyn Park. His methods included preserving and incorporating as great a number of local plants, shrubs, and trees into his designs as possible. As a result, a large number of original trees were preserved during construction, including sycamore, red oak, white oak, and maple trees. After securing deeds to the land from private properties, construction began on the parkway on

October 14, 1903. Teams of horses were used to drag logs up the steep inclines, and the rest of the work was done by hand labor through the rough weeds and difficult terrain. Lookout areas were constructed to allow visitors to observe the picturesque view and natural beauty without disturbing traffic. The two-and-a-half-mile driveway park was an immediate success with both local townspeople and visitors. Initially the roadway was in very poor shape, with deep ruts and potholes making navigation difficult. Dust was also a problem. A paving program was later implemented in 1936 that was successful in making the road more traversable.

Grandview Drive was designed for pedestrian, horse, and automobile use and was the testing ground for the first gasoline-powered automobile in America, the Duryea automobile. Pres. Theodore Roosevelt visited Peoria in October 1910 and took a carriage ride to the Peoria Country Club via Grandview Drive. After his country club visit, President Roosevelt was driven back down the hill toward the city, and one of the men in his group apologized for the poor state of the road. President Roosevelt remarked, "What difference does it make? I have traveled all over the world, and this is the world's most beautiful drive." Since that time, Grandview Drive has been known as the "World's Most Beautiful Drive," and in 1927, Peoria's first radio station adopted the call letters of WMBD in honor of the World's Most Beautiful Drive. A bridge, pavilion, World War I monument, the Peoria Country Club, and Grandview Park are located within the Grandview Drive Historic District, an area encompassing over 180 acres.

A plaque was placed on Grandview Drive to honor the earliest explorers in the area and reads, "Pimiteoui Meaning 'Fat Lake' Illinois Indian Name for Peoria Lake. Here Passed Joliet and Marquette in 1673, Established Near The Lake Were Ft. Crevecouer 1680. Ft. St. Louis 1691-92; Old Peoria's Fort and Village, 1730; Peoria's 1778; Ft. Clark, 1813; French Trading House 'Opa Post', Before 1816. Americans Settled on the Site of the City of Peoria in 1819. Peorians are living in the oldest settlement within the boundaries of Illinois."

Grandview Drive continues to inspire admiration from those walking or driving along the bluffs just as it first did during construction. The driveway retains its original design, and little has changed in its 90-plus-year history. There are breathtaking views of the Illinois River, and the valley below the bluffs has been preserved by the Peoria Park District. This area remains undeveloped to allow the natural scenery to flourish.

Grandview Drive has been the site of many ghost stories over the years. The following article was taken from the *Peoria Herald* dated April 13, 1907:

> The town was agog over the presence of a ghost that haunted Grandview Drive almost nightly and chased its victims along the road. A group of townspeople went up to investigate and saw the thing travel after dark down the hairpin curve hill. Young couples no longer pulled their sporty rigs up in the evening shadows along the drive to contemplate the moon and view, avoiding the spot in fear of the dreaded specter. The specter usually took off after its intended prey as it started up the hill, but it always disappeared before the top was reached. No one admitted having fallen victim, although one hapless man was found beaten and bruised on the hill one night and thought he might have been the victim of the ghost's attacks. The police were called and disagreed with this assessment, arresting the man for drunk and disorderly behavior. On the night of April 16, 1907, Frank Baldwin and Charlie May, two skeptics, reported they drove their horse and buggy over to disprove the story, but instead they were convinced the ghost had attempted to run them down, and they had seen the white form with their own eyes floating back into the woods. Townspeople speculated this was the ghost of a man who had recently killed his wife and whose own corpse was believed to be lying somewhere in the underbrush. Although later boys had rigged up a sheet with a wire, the sightings continued.

Since that time, Grandview Drive has continued to delight local citizens and visitors with its grand vistas and has also continued to generate tales of ghosts along the roadway. Local legend holds that a young couple, out for a drive along the road at night, failed to navigate a curve along Grandview Drive and crashed into the valley below. The girl was killed instantly. Since that time, there have been reports of the figure of a young girl in a white dress, seen wandering in the woods at the valley where she was killed. If anyone approaches, the figure simply disappears into the night. There are also reports of strange green balls of light seen shooting through the woods. No source for these lights has been discovered.

Kickapoo

Nearby Jubilee College and a short drive from Peoria is the small town of Kickapoo. That quaint village has some ghost stories and legends of its own. The following excerpt was taken from the *Peoria Herald* on June 14, 1855:

> Magic curative powers were credited to the mad stone owned by Dr. James Lewis of Kickapoo. The stone had been applied by the doctor to dog bite wounds received by Peter Rider from a mad dog. The application was made 58 hours after the dog bite. Then the stone was dropped in sweet milk to complete the cure. Rider had no ill effects from the bite, although they knew the dog was mad because a little boy it had previously bitten had died in agony from rabies and a hog had gone the same way.

In addition to magical cures, Kickapoo is home to local spirits that plague its citizenry. The following excerpt was taken from the local paper on March 27, 1859:

> The newspaper reading population was considerably upset about a ghost in the neighboring village of Kickapoo who had acquired the habit of sitting on the legs of his affinities. The Thing was first noticed some three months before when it appeared in the home of a reputable family of the village. The grandfather was alone that night, and had gone to bed to ease his rheumatism. Lying there by himself with the moonlight streaming in the window, he awoke to find a weight pressing on his legs. At first, he thought the dog had climbed on the bed and was sleeping there, but a glance showed him this was not true. Fearing he was becoming paralyzed he threw off the covers and stepped to the floor. His limbs were as good as ever–barring the rheumatism. He returned to bed and almost immediately the pressure was back. Again, he climbed out of bed, felt the pressure leave, returned to bed, and found it back again. Within a few hours the family returned and learned of the happenings. The son, a mature man, climbed in the bed to try out the phenomenon and experienced the same feeling as the father. That night the two slept together with the Thing pressing down on their legs. Next day, a son from Peoria came out and heard of the strange happenings. He scoffed at the story, but after spending one night in the bed felt the same invisible weight pressing down on him and agreed the room was haunted. Now after three months of the sort of goings on, the mystery was deeper than ever. It was noted that no noises had been heard at any time other then when the moon shone into the room. When the light struck the bedroom, the family members reported they saw a dark figure glide around the room wearing a cowl and long, loose gown.

Lacon

One popular explanation for the presence of ghosts is the need to avenge a wrong, particularly a wrongful death. In an article in the local weekly in Peoria on November 14, 1896, it was noted that a particularly egregious incident had led to reports of ghost sightings. An African American male, formerly a resident of Peoria and Toluca, had been accused of attacking and injuring a white woman on November 7, 1896. Bloodhounds were employed to chase the unfortunate man through the nearby marshes, and he was eventually captured and taken to the Lacon jail. The man pleaded for his release, repeatedly proclaiming his innocence, but according to law enforcement officials, he eventually confessed to the assault from his jail cell. Following his arrest, a mob of local miners assembled and donned masks. They approached the entrance to the jail and demanded the prisoner be handed over to mob justice. The local sheriff apparently refused, as he was later found locked in a jail cell.

The unfortunate man was taken by the mob by horseback to the outskirts of town to a large white oak tree. A noose was fashioned and he was hung from the tree. The mob disbanded shortly thereafter, and the whereabouts of the body remain unknown. Sheriff Paskell claimed that he could not recognize any members of the mob that had murdered the man, and no one was ever arrested or tried for the crime. However, there was a different kind of justice. Shortly after the death, prisoners in the jail began to report sightings of an African American male in a cell in the jailhouse. The fear became intense, and many prisoners requested transfer to a different facility to avoid the ghost. Sheriff Paskell said several prisoners had pleaded with him to take them to another jail or even to prison rather than leave them at the mercy of the nocturnal specter. The spirit, unable to avenge the wrongs of life, was rumored to have remained at the local jail to avenge himself after death.

Dickson Mounds State Park

Located just outside Lewistown and a short drive from Peoria are the Dickson Mounds, a group of mound-shaped graves that hold the bones of hundreds of Native Americans from the region.

The early Paleolithic Indians in the Illinois River valley received the name of Mound Builders because ceremonial burial mounds were one of the chief characteristics of the people. The mounds are supposed to have been built as places of religious worship, and those who built them were generally thought to have been sun worshippers. The mounds also served as ceremonial temples and ultimately burial places for Native Americans. From around 1,000 BC, the Late Woodland–era Native Americans in central Illinois buried their dead in the first mounds, located near the intersection of Illinois and Spoon Rivers in Fulton County. Around AD 800, the Native Americans of the Mississippian tribes lived in a large village located on the flat areas to the north of present-day Dickson Mounds. The village included an open plaza and ceremonial structure. The Mississippians occupied this area until around AD 1200, when the people inexplicably vanished. Various possibilities for their disappearance exist, including warfare, major climatic change, or epidemics of disease that might have decimated the population. Regardless, these people left behind an extraordinary collection of artifacts and burial sites. Some common characteristics of the Mississippian culture include public and communal architecture, flat-topped mounds, occasional practice of human sacrifice, and creation and ornamentation of vessels made from pottery, shell, and stone. These traits suggest a hierarchical society and complex social and political system.

Burials at the Dickson excavation closely resemble patterns of the Middle Mississippian movement. The graves were originally built into the side of a preexisting hill on the bluff edge of the village. At a later date, mounds were added at the site, and the graves were built into the side of the man-made mounds. There is also evidence of former pits or mass graves, where bodies were likely left to decompose for a time prior to burial, perhaps during the winter months. Over half the graves also contain evidence of goods buried along with the body. Burial activity at Dickson Mounds began in AD 1000 and ended sometime in the mid-1300s, coinciding with the disappearance of the Cahokia people in the area. The final graves are

Native American burial remains were discovered at Dickson Mounds in 1927. (Courtesy of the Illinois State Historical Society.)

predominantly mass graves, which would suggest some form of illness or plague in the area that precluded individual burials. The soil in this area is rich in calcium oxide and ideal for the preservation of these ancient remains.

The land of Dickson Mounds was originally designated as a military tract and was laid out following the War of 1812 to be given to soldiers as payment for war service. Amateur excavations in the 1800s at the site resulted in the loss of a large number of pottery and burial artifacts. The area containing the mounds was purchased by the John Eveland family around 1814. In 1833, William Dickson moved from Kentucky to Illinois and bought the land to construct a farm and orchard. In cultivating the land in the 1860s, the farmer discovered a number of Native American artifacts such as fishhooks, spear points, and scraping knives. They also discovered that the mounds held the bodies of Native Americans. Word of this discovery spread quickly, and the remains quickly became a tourist destination for the farming families in the local community.

In 1927, William Dickson's son Don F. Dickson began excavations on the farm he owned 45 miles southwest of Peoria. He had an interest in archaeology and recognized the historical and anthropological significance of the burial mounds on the grounds of his farm. He uncovered graves beneath the soil but did not remove or disarrange the bones or artifacts. He placed a tent over the site to protect the area and opened the dig site to the public. In the 1930s, archaeologists from the University of Chicago excavated the site. There had been disturbance of the burial area, and the original shape was somewhat altered and almost leveled in some areas. In addition, some of the mounds were destroyed around 1900 where excavations were made to construct farm outbuildings. There was also displacement of bones due to tree roots and erosion, resulting in the crushing of most of the skulls of children under 12 years old. Despite this, the composition of the soil had preserved the skeletal remains in a nearly perfect condition.

The first burials at the site were pit burials or were made by carving vaults into the side of naturally occurring hills. When these sites were no longer sufficient, burial mounds were constructed. There are more than 90 burials at the site, holding 248 skeletons. There are 11 separate burial mounds and a mortuary mound. Tributes or gifts were placed within the graves, such as jewelry, knives, and tool kits. Eating equipment was uncovered with small children, indicating it had been made for them but never used due to the untimely deaths. Artifacts were placed on the shoulders, head, chest, or between the knees. The distribution of gifts was gender specific; the males were buried with clackers, bone hairpins, shell-bead bracelets, and pipes, and the females were buried with bead necklaces and antler rings. There is evidence the bodies were tightly bound for burial, although few remnants of this wrapping remain. Causes of death were attributed to bone disease, injuries, and old age. The average age of the deceased individuals was 42 for males and 35 for females.

After the excavations, Don F. Dickson replaced the tent with a building he opened as a private museum. The museum was an instant success, as visitors poured in from surrounding towns and cities. Following World War II, Dickson sold the site to the State of Illinois but remained as manager of the museum. In 1965, the site was transferred to the Illinois State Museum, and the present museum opened to the public in 1972. Native American groups around the country objected to the site, which they claimed displayed the bones in a manner deemed offensive. The state negotiated with Native American groups, and a compromise was reached when the burial closed to the public on April 3, 1992. The 30-by-60-foot Dickson excavation covers only one-tenth of the total area of the cemetery complex.

At the 230-acre site today, the remains of three ceremonial Mississippian buildings are on display, along with two cemeteries and 10 mounds. It is believed that, prior to modern explorations, there may have been more than 3,000 individuals buried at the site. There is also an observation deck that offers sweeping vistas of the surrounding countryside.

This is sacred ground, and many visiting the site have reported a unique energy in the area, a sense of harmony and peace coming from the grounds. Photographs taken at the site often reveal strange swirling mists or balls of light. There have also been stories that those with heightened psychic awareness have contacted the spirits of some of the souls resting here. The Native American community looks upon ancestor spirits with respect and fear, and Dickson Mounds represents the final resting ground for those at peace. This burial site remains a powerful and moving reminder of the history of the central Illinois Native American community in the area.

Starved Rock State Park and Lodge

Leaving the ghostly confines of Peoria and driving toward the north, a visitor to central Illinois would come across an area of singular beauty and awe-inspiring natural vistas. The Starved Rock State Park in Utica consists of a series of rugged peaks that were carved into the Illinois bluffs by glaciers over 5,000 years ago. The site between the Vermilion and Illinois Rivers offers picturesque views and challenging hiking trails in the heart of central Illinois farmland. A sandstone rock rises abruptly from the riverbank and climbs over 160 feet. Its summit is more than half an acre in diameter, and visitors to the site can enjoy virtually the same breathtaking view as was enjoyed by the original settlers.

This area in the Illinois Valley was formerly the site of the largest confederation of Native Americans in the United States. The Illinois Confederacy was made up of the following tribes: the Cahokias, the Kaskaskias, the Tamaroas, the Peorias, and the Michigamies. These tribes welcomed the first French settlers into Illinois in the early 1600s, eager to take advantage of the goods the newcomers brought with them to trade for fur and game.

Jacques Marquette and Louis Joliet paddled down the shores of Lake Michigan in 1673. They were on an expedition to find a new trade route to China. They eventually found themselves at the north end of the Illinois River. While traveling inland one day, the visitors entered the Native American village of La Vamtum, or Kaskaskia, near the present-day town of Utica. The village contained 460 cabins; long open buildings covered by double mats of material. Up to 10 families lived within each of the cabins. The Kaskaskia welcomed the weary explorers, and Marquette vowed to return to the village after their expedition. He kept his word, returning to the Illini village and founding the Mission of the Immaculate Conception in 1675. Father Marquette stayed with the mission for a short time, converting as many of the local Native Americans to Christianity as possible. He died on his return to Canada.

In 1681, Robert Cavalier de LaSalle and his lieutenant Henri Tonti came across the Illini village while on a mission to build a chain of forts for King Louis XIV to prevent the English from moving westward. The Frenchmen found the large rock in the bluff and decided it would be a good vantage point if they were ever under attack by hostile tribes. They cut away the forest at the summit in order to construct a crude fort and named the post Fort St. Louis du Rocher after King Louis XIV. LaSalle and Tonti then returned to their mission, eventually building Fort Creve Couer in Peoria in 1680. The fort at Starved Rock was later abandoned and burned by the local Native Americans in 1718.

The area was left virtually untouched until the advancing English fought with Native Americans in 1765. Pontiac, a Native American ally to the French explorers, fought savagely against the English. On a trip to Cahokia in 1769, he was murdered, allegedly by a member of the Illinois tribe, for the bribe of a barrel of whiskey. The Potawatomi, Kickapoo, and Miami tribes sought revenge on the Illini men and women for the death of Pontiac and waged a brutal massacre on the plains. The population of the Illinois at Starved Rock was reduced to half, and the remnants of the battered Illini tribe huddled on the top of the huge rock. When the warrior tribes returned, the Illini found themselves trapped at the apex. The war raged on and the Illini fought valiantly for their lives. The struggle continued over the course of several days. The sides of the rock glistened red with the blood of their comrades who had fallen over the precipice and those left bloody and dying at the top. The Potawatomi, Kickapoo, and Miami formed an encampment at the base of the rock in the meadow and gave no quarter to anyone attempting to descend. They watched and waited. As the need for water grew, the Illini formed crude buckskin buckets and attempted to lower them down into the river. The tribes waiting below saw the buckets descending and cruelly cut the ropes, thus effectively ensuring the Illini would die slowly and painfully of exposure, dehydration, and starvation. The victors ascended the rock and killed the few remaining members of the Illini tribe still left with their hatchets.

A few days after the massacre, a group of traders was passing through the area and saw buzzards circling the top of the rock. They walked up to the apex and encountered the butchered and bloated remains of the Illini, rotting in the sun, their carcasses slowly picked apart by vultures. The smell of the scene was overwhelming, and the group lost no time in getting back to their canoes and heading north toward Canada. With them, these traders took the story of the brave Illini tribe and the legend of the bloodstained Starved Rock.

Settlers slowly pushed their way across the Illinois Valley, settling and farming the land and taking advantage of the varied abundance of wildlife. The construction of the Illinois and Michigan Canal in the 1840s brought with it laborers and traders. The waterway was across from Starved Rock and was instrumental in drawing settlers to the area. Col. Daniel F. Hitt was a Civil War officer and surveyor and became the first civilian owner of Starved Rock, purchasing the land from the federal government on June 23, 1835. Colonel Hitt was well aware of the history of the Native American tribes in the area, as well as the legend of Starved Rock. He created historical records and maps of the area, and presented the various Native American artifacts he uncovered on his land. Colonel Hitt sold Starved Rock and the surrounding land to Ferdinand Walter in 1890 for $21,000.

The area was slowly becoming a visitor destination due to its natural beauty and history. Two local men, William Osman Jr. and Horace Hull, recognized the importance of preservation of this site and campaigned for the state to purchase and manage the property. The Illinois General Assembly authorized $146,000 to be paid to Mr. and Mrs. Ferdinand Walter in 1911. The new Starved Rock State Park was born. A hotel was built near the rock, offering a swimming pool and dance hall. A ferry boat and paved roads made it more convenient for tourists to enjoy the beauty of the area.

In 1930, the country entered the Great Depression, and state funding for parks and projects virtually disappeared. In response, the federal government created the Civilian Conservation Corps (CCC) to provide work for the many unemployed and aid states in preserving historic sites and monuments. Two CCC companies worked at Starved Rock, performing maintenance of the trails and buildings.

The economy recovered, and the area increased in popularity as a vacation destination. The present-day Starved Rock Lodge and log cabins were built to accommodate the growing number of tourists to the area. The buildings were constructed on a bluff overlooking Starved Rock, and the future of the site as a tourism mecca was ensured.

The Starved Rock Murders

On Monday, March 14, 1960, Frances Murphy, Mildred Lindquist, and Lillian Oetting traveled from their respective homes in Riverside to spend a four-day holiday at Starved Rock State Park.

Lindquist and Oetting were 50 years old, and Murphy was 47. The three were affluent, well educated, and active at their church, the Presbyterian Church of Riverside. They also shared a love of nature and outdoor activities. Oetting had spent the previous winter caring for her husband, who was recovering from a heart attack, and the three women were eager to take a vacation.

Oetting had promised to telephone her husband every evening after the group returned to the lodge. When the call did not come through Monday night, Mr. Oetting called the lodge. He could not reach the women and presumed they were out for the evening. Tuesday morning, Mr. Oetting once again attempted to reach his wife. The desk clerk mistakenly believed the three women had eaten breakfast in the lodge that morning but had left for the afternoon. Greatly relieved, Mr. Oetting left a message and resolved to speak with his wife that evening.

Mr. Oetting called the lodge again early Wednesday morning. No longer satisfied with assurances from the desk clerk, he demanded that someone go to his wife's room to check on her. An inspection of the rooms was not comforting. The women's bags had all been found unpacked, and none of the beds appeared to have been slept in. Mr. Oetting was alarmed and asked if Murphy's car, a gray station wagon, was still in the parking lot. The car was still there and was covered in a layer of ice and snow that made it clear the car had not been moved since the snowstorm on Tuesday. Mr. Oetting was frantic and telephoned the husbands of Frances Murphy and Mildred Lindquist. Those two gentlemen immediately left Riverside to drive to Starved Rock Lodge. They would arrive late on Wednesday, after the official search was well under way. Mr. Oetting was still recovering from his heart attack and forbidden to travel, but the pair promised him an update upon their arrival at the lodge.

Mr. Oetting next placed a call to Virgil Peterson, director of the Chicago Crime Commission and a friend to all three families. Peterson telephoned the Illinois State Police to jump-start the search for the women, and within minutes, Sheriff Ray Eutsey of the LaSalle County Sheriff's Department had organized search parties and sent them to the park. Local news reporter Bill Danley had gotten word of the missing women and was already in the park. He came across a group of youths from the Illinois Youth Commission Forest Camp who breathlessly exclaimed they had come across the bodies of three partially clothed women in the park. Danley went and called Sheriff Eutsey before proceeding back into the park. Most of the search parties believed the women had gotten lost, or in the worst case, had died from exposure or a fall from a ledge. No one looking for the women could even imagine they would be the victims of mass homicide.

Danley and the youth commission group took the trail leading back to the St. Louis canyon. They stopped abruptly upon reaching a small cave to the south of the trail. The bodies of the three women, battered and bloodied, lay on the cave floor. The cave was set in a rock wall, so the bodies were at eye level from the trail. All three women were lying on the their backs, their heads and faces so brutally beaten their features were nearly unrecognizable. The lower half of their clothing was missing. Lindquist's bloody camera lay 10 feet from her body.

The state police arrived and immediately cordoned off the trail and the small cave to preserve evidence. A preliminary search of the canyon floor revealed blood stains and smears, evidence that a violent struggle had taken place. The binoculars the group had used were shattered and bloodstained, and a broken, frozen tree limb lying near the bodies was thought to be a potential murder weapon. Police cameramen took photographs from every imaginable angle, trying to preserve the scene for use at a future trial.

Later in the afternoon as the investigation continued, Mr. Lindquist and Mr. Murphy approached the scene. None of the investigators were aware of their presence until the two men broke down into tears at the sight of the battered bodies still lying on the frozen ground. They immediately turned away and made their way back down the trail, sobbing silently into the cold March air.

As the local community learned of the gruesome crime, visitors began hurriedly checking out of the lodge. Local citizens bought locks and bolted their doors, and women did not travel out alone. The locals avoided going near the park, fearing the killer was still on the grounds, bloodstained, crazed, and ready to kill again.

Fifty people that were at or near the lodge at the time the women disappeared were interrogated and subject to polygraph testing. Everyone passed the test. Among those questioned was

21-year-old Chester Weger, a kitchen worker at the lodge. Weger told police that he was in the basement of the lodge on the day of the murder tending the furnace and writing a letter to his girlfriend Patricia Sandys. Although a statement from the lodge caretaker indicated that Weger had gotten a ride with Stanley Tucker to Oglesby that afternoon, Weger denied that and claimed he had remained in the lodge. Stanley Tucker also denied going anywhere with Weger that day. Although it was noted that Weger had some cuts on his face during the interview, he explained that he had cut himself shaving. Weger was questioned a total of four times, but there was no evidence linking him to the murder.

A $35,000 reward for information related to the murders was offered by the families of the murdered women. This generated the submission of tips from people all over the country. Two women, Colleen Thorton and Vicki Templeton, came forward and related a robbery attempt that had occurred to them in Starved Rock in July 1959. The information was filed away. The police also received a letter from a lawyer in Chicago. He had two clients who encountered a strange man at the St. Louis canyon icefall on March 12, 1960. The women were shaken by the encounter and felt the young man would have injured them, but they had a young child with them. Both women identified a photograph of Chester Weger as the man they had encountered.

The search continued in the park. On April 2, 1960, Sgt. Michael Frankovich of the Illinois State Police recovered small slips of pink paper that had been exposed in the spring thaw. The scraps proved to be part of a letter written on Starved Rock stationery to someone named Pat. The scraps were found on a trail nearly 100 feet above the crime scene.

As spring turned into summer, the investigation grew stale. With no definite evidence or leads, the police continued to scour the grounds of the park, looking for any evidence that could provide a new lead.

The Confession

State's attorney Harland Warren took most of the criticism for the failure of the case. Warren took matters into his own hands and launched a personal investigation in July 1960. Warren collected all existing evidence and data and reexamined all evidence. Warren asked Sheriff Ray Eutsey to give him two deputies who could be relied on for their discretion. Warren sent the pictures the women had taken during their hike for analysis of shadows at that time to determine a more precise time of death. The expert concluded the photographs had been taken at approximately 2:30 p.m. Using the time of the photographs and the path the women would have taken at the trail, Warren and his two deputies estimated the time of the attack around 3:15 to 3:30 p.m. Warren returned to the lodge to see if the twine that had been used to bind the women together had come from the lodge. He found twine matching the twine count of both samples in the lodge kitchen. Warren ordered new polygraph tests of all lodge employees beginning on September 22, 1960.

Chester Weger was questioned for 15 minutes on Monday, September 26, 1960. Weger was then requested to go to a specialist in polygraph in Chicago and readily acquiesced. Weger and Warren went to Chicago on September 27, 1960. Weger failed the lie detector tests. Warren asked for Weger's leather jacket to run further tests, and Weger again readily agreed. Warren sent the jacket to the FBI laboratory in Washington, D.C. The FBI laboratory concluded that blood found on Weger's jacket was human blood.

At the same time, deputies recollected a rape and robbery in Matthieson State Park in 1959. They took mug shots to the couple, and the woman identified Chester Weger as the assailant.

On November 16, 1960, Warren ordered deputies Bill Dummett and Wayne Hess to bring Weger in for questioning. Weger smoked cigarettes steadily as he once again denied being in the park the day of the murders and denied any involvement in the crime. He claimed the torn pieced of pink paper that had been his love letter to Pat had been thrown into the canyon at various times over the course of a few weeks. He again claimed the scratches of his face were the result of a shaving accident. Weger also revealed he was aware of the location of the twine kept in the kitchen and had used it to show some rope tricks to colleagues at work. As the deputies finished their questions regarding the triple murder, they asked Weger about the rape of the young girl on September 13, 1959, and the robbery of the girl and her boyfriend. He was also questioned about another rape when he was a juvenile.

Weger withstood the questioning until 8:00 p.m. without a break in his reserve or calm. Warren had arranged a lineup with the victims of the 1959 rape and robbery, and Weger was picked from the lineup without hesitation. Weger was charged with the crime.

The deputies continued to question Weger, who eventually broke down and began to cry when questioned about his wife and family. The police called Weger's parents and wife, who came and visited him in the interrogation room. His parents implored him to tell the truth. Weger finally broke down and confessed.

The Crime

Chester Weger described the triple homicide in detail for the deputies. He reported that on March 14, 1960, he had approached Frances Murphy, Mildred Lindquist, and Lillian Oetting as they turned to leave the St. Louis Canyon. Murphy was in the lead, carrying the binoculars around her neck. They started to cross a small bridge about 250 feet from the canyon when Weger approached them and walked toward them on the trail. Weger thought the binoculars and camera the women were carrying were handbags. Weger approached the women walking, but at the bridge made a lunge for Oetting and tried to get her camera case. As Oetting struggled with Weger, the strap of the camera broke and Weger grabbed the case. The other women approached him, and Murphy struck him with the binoculars, bruising his right eye, and raked his face with a hair comb. Lindquist yelled at Weger to stop and grabbed the camera back from him. Weger grabbed Murphy by the wrists and looked at the three women. Weger told them he would not hurt them and if they went back to the waterfall at the canyon and agreed to let him tie them up. The three women were distrustful but, according to Weger, reluctantly agreed to this course of action. He led them into the canyon and pulled the twine he had taken from the kitchen from his back pocket. He tied the three women together by the wrists and ankles. According to Weger, he started to walk away, getting about 75 feet from the canyon. At that moment, Weger claimed that Murphy pulled herself free and ran after him, striking him in the back of the head. Weger claimed he then grabbed a frozen tree limb and hit Murphy repeatedly in the head and face. He then picked her up and carried her inert body back to the two horrified women back in the canyon. Weger then walked back out and brought the club into the cave. Weger claimed that the other women tried to stand up as he approached. Weger took the club and struck Oetting and Lindquist in the face and head. He also used the camera and the binoculars in the attack. Weger then claimed that Murphy got up and hit him again with the binoculars. He ran after her, striking her to the ground with his fist and then again hitting her repeatedly until he was sure she was dead. After he had felt for pulses on his victims, Weger claimed he saw a single-engine plane flying overhead and wanted to make sure the three bodies were not spotted from the air. He dragged the three women into the cave above the canyon. He pulled up the skirts of the women and ripped off their underwear to make it look as though the three women had been raped. He went through their coats and pockets but could find no money on them. He washed his hands and pants with snow and left the dead women in the approaching twilight. Weger told the police that when he returned to the lodge it was almost 5:00 p.m.

Weger finished his confession at 3:00 a.m. Following the confession, Harland Warren made the decision to take the prisoner out to St. Louis canyon in order to get a confession at the scene and pinpoint exactly where the various points of the attack had taken place. Weger agreed to the trip and slept soundly in his cell until it was time to go. The police and Warren, eager to redeem themselves in the eyes of the public for the allegedly botched investigation, contacted news reporters to inform them of the upcoming field trip. Journalists photographed Weger as he was led to a black unmarked county car. It was a cold morning as the large group trooped toward St. Louis canyon. Halfway there, Weger stopped and pointed out the upper trail he had taken into and out of the area. Weger identified the spot on the footbridge where he had encountered the women and how he forced them back into the canyon. He described in brutal detail how he had bludgeoned the women to death, ripped off their clothing, and then dragged them up into the cave to avoid discovery. He then took the group back to the lodge. Weger was taken from the park and returned to his cell at the county jail. Weger was interviewed almost constantly over the next two days and repeated his confession.

On November 18, 1960, a grand jury indictment charged Weger with three counts of murder, as well as assault, rape, and robbery from the incident on September 13, 1959. To ensure the case was airtight, Warren had his deputies searched for the owner of the single-engine plane that had flown overhead following the murders. Weger was found guilty, and the 1961 trial ended in a life sentence for Weger.

The Aftermath

Appeals for the Lillian Oetting conviction kept Weger from facing previous murder charges until 1963. By that time, the prosecution was precluded under Illinois law from proceeding with the rape and robbery charge from 1959, due to speedy trial provisions. It was clear to the state that another murder charge would inflict no further punishment on the defendant, since, according to Judge Ryan, the second murder charge would run concurrently with the first. Weger would remain in prison for the murder of Lillian Oetting.

The Starved Rock Murder reward had risen to a little over $38,000. Harland Warren received over $10,000 of that fund for solving the murders. The rest was distributed to the two deputies Warren had used in his investigation and to civilians who had provided information that led to Weger's eventual conviction. Warren died on May 20, 2007, at the age of 90.

Charles Weger continued to pursue parole from his Western Correctional Center cell. He was last denied parole by the prisoner review board on September 25, 2008. Weger has never shown any remorse for his crime.

The Ghosts of Starved Rock

There are a number of spirits that are said the roam the ragged peaks and bluffs of Starved Rock, including legends that at least one of the murdered women from the 1960 murders still inhabits St. Louis Canyon. Visitors to the site say they are disturbed by the sound of strange moans and sudden icy cold spots in the area. One visitor related how he and his friend had been visiting the park and attempted to take the same route as the murdered women. As they were leaving St. Louis Canyon, there was a rush of wind that stirred the still day, sweeping past them toward the exit. At the same time, they caught a glimpse of a white figure running across the canyon floor. There have also been reports of the sound of footsteps on the bridge near the canyon.

The Starved Rock legend of the Illini plunging to their deaths or dying of starvation seized the public imagination when the park was first built in 1911. There are stories that the blood from the massacre is still visible running down the cliffs and that the cries and laments of the Illini slowing perishing on the sandstone can still be heard in the howl of the wind. Some claim to have seen the apparition of an Illini warrior standing at the top of the peak, looking out toward the scenic valley. There are also frequent reports of Native American war cries, echoing through the night and bouncing through the canyons.

One particular tale involves a pair of young Native American lovers. The Lover's Leap legend of Starved Rock tells of a boy from the Illinois tribe who fell in love with a Kaskaskia maiden. Neither side of the family would allow the union, so the pair set off on foot, confident that they could start a new life together. They only made it as far as the cliff at Lover's Leap. The pair vowed that if they could not be together always, they did not want to live. In a fatal suicide pact, they joined hands and leapt from Lover's Leap to the jagged rocks below, remaining together forever at Starved Rock. There is a legend at Starved Rock that the footprints of both the young lovers can be seen at the top of the rock, and on the anniversary of their death, their images will appear and make that fatal leap again.

If there are Native American spirits left at the site, they are not alone. There are rumors that Al Capone used the park as his own personal playground, and that over 40 bodies of his murdered victims were thrown down shafts, holes, and into caverns. If restless ghosts seek a proper burial, then Starved Rock is definitely the site of troubled spirits. There are stories of visitors hearing voices in the caverns and seeing shadowy figures emerge and disappear from the caves.

To this day, there are legends that Henri Tonti's gold is buried somewhere at the top of Starved Rock, and that Tonti himself left clues as the whereabouts in natural features around the area. In the park's early years, treasure seekers from all over the state would come to dig at the site and attempt to uncover the missing cache. The park is under legal safeguard from scavengers today, so no excavating is permitted. Tonti's gold remains intact and protected.

It is a popular belief that the lodge itself is built on the site of Native American burial grounds. There are reports of lights turning on and off in lodge rooms and of televisions mysteriously turning on in the middle of the night. Employees have also reported hearing the sounds of clinking china, music, and laughter coming from the lodge dining room long after the room is closed for the evening. Many here believe that a ghostly party continues in the dining room after the lights at the lodge have gone out.

Since its first discovery in the 1600s, Starved Rock State Park continues to enchant visitors with its haunting beauty and breathtaking natural views. Even those not fortunate enough to have an encounter with the supernatural can still leave the site with a sense of wonder that such scenery could exist in the flat farmland of central Illinois. If visiting, please allow a full day as some of the trails are demanding and the views demand time to relax and soak in the glorious scenery.

Eleven

GHOSTS OF THE ILLINOIS RIVER

Presently a film of dark smoke appears above one of those remote 'points';
instantly a Negro drayman, famous for his quick eye and prodigious voice, lifts up the cry,
'S-t-e-a-m-b-o-a-t-a-comin'!' and the scene changes! The town drunkard stirs, the clerks wake up, a
furious clatter of drays follows, every house and store pours out a human contribution,
and all in a twinkling the dead town is alive and moving. Drays, carts, men, boys
all go hurrying from many quarters to a common center, the wharf.
—Mark Twain, *Life on the Mississippi*

The Illinois River was formed by the convergence of the Des Plaines and Kankakee Rivers. It is over 270 miles long and snakes through the heart of the state, eventually emptying itself into the Mississippi River. The waterway has been a vital means of transportation and commerce, from the first Native Americans paddling birch bark canoes, to the later barges that transported goods downstream to New Orleans. Early traders used canoes or crude flat boats to carry pelts to Canada and brought back Native American goods such as blankets, beads, gunpowder, guns, and knives. These goods were used by the trappers and hunters to create the peltry for trade.

In 1673, Louis Joliet wrote that the Illinois River could become an important navigational link in commerce and travel if a canal were dug to connect the Des Plaines River with the Chicago River thereby creating a waterway between Lake Michigan and the Illinois River. In the meantime, traders, trappers, and hunters used the waterway for canoes and rowboats to expand their trading westward.

The first steamboat appeared on the Illinois River in 1819 or 1820, and Peoria quickly became the site of extensive boat construction. Builders such as William Moss and Tobias Bradley ran their steamboats, packet boats, towboats, and steam propellers up and down the river. The boats were used to transport the household furnishing, foodstuffs, and clothing demanded by the burgeoning river town. The early steamboat boilers burned wood, and each boat used one cord of wood every 24 hours for each ton of weight. To support this consumption, the banks of the Illinois River teemed with wood yards, where the steamboats could buy wood for $1.50 to $5 per cord, depending on the season.

From 1829, when the first steamboat arrived, until 1854, when the first railroad began operating, the Illinois River was the primary means of conveying people and merchandise to and from the city. By 1837, steamboats arrived at Peoria on a regular basis, up to 150 per year. There were 17 packet lines in service as of 1840, with owners competing to take control of the waterway. The most famous of the steamboat dynasties was that of David M. Swain, who along with his family built and ran both packet and excursion boats on the Illinois River from 1880 to 1930. Many of these steamboats were dubbed "floating palaces," with mahogany bars, gleaming brass fixtures, crystal chandeliers, luxurious carpets, and every available amenity to enhance the pleasure and comfort of those on board. There was imported wine and fine dining in the elaborate dining areas and cafés.

Between 1850 and 1860, steamboat excursions reached their peak of popularity. The residents of early Peoria would flock to the waterfront when the first strains of the calliope rang sweetly in the sky, awaiting the arrival of the next excursion boat. At that time, the waterfront was undeveloped, and those standing on the shore were separated from the giant boats by only a few short gangplanks set into the mud. Steamboat watching was as popular of a sport as actually boarding the boats, and the Peoria waterfront was a hub of energy and activity during the long, hot summers. In 1856, there were up to 70 boats anchored at the Peoria dock at one time. The rate for a passenger cabin from Peoria to St. Louis was $6 for the all-expense-paid, two-week trip. Steamboats originally traveled from 6 to 8 miles per hour, but by the end of the golden era of steamboats, they were moving up to 20 miles per hour. There were many steamboat races held for recreation, resulting in a number of accidents and injuries. Competition for passengers on board the ships was fierce, and one local steamboat rivalry resulted in shots being fired as the boats passed at close range on the river.

Congress passed laws that resulted in the completion of the Illinois and Michigan Canal in 1848. In 1858, the Illinois River Packet Company was organized to run on the Illinois River and remained in operation until 1867. The Great Lakes-to-Gulf Deep Waterway opened on June 20, 1933. This was a complex system of locks on the Illinois River that went into operation, making the river fully navigable by large towboats and barges. The packet lines quickly gave way to giant barges pushed by tugboats that could carry huge amounts of cargo. These gentle giants lumber up and down the Illinois River to this day.

Since the first explorations by Jacques Marquette and Louis Joliet, there have been stories of ghosts and legends surrounding the Illinois River and area waterways. The murky waters have been the scene of many tragedies, which have spawned superstitions and folklore. These tales have survived since the time the first Peorians occupied a village at the base of Peoria Lake and continue to fascinate those enjoying the waterway today.

The Sinking of the *Columbia*

In the early 20th century, the steamboat excursion business was thriving on the Illinois River, with riverboats offering daytime and evening cruises with food, drinks, and dancing. A steamboat would arrive at river towns such Peoria and play cheerful music from its steam calliope to alert locals of its arrival. Thousands flocked to the riverfront to board the popular excursion boats of the time. The *East St. Louis*, the *Julia Belle Swain*, the *Idlewood*, and the *Columbia* all plied their trade. The boats had a capacity to carry 600 to 1,200 people per trip, and the riverboat captains and pilots found themselves in a booming trade. One of the most popular steamers for residents of Peoria and Pekin was the *Columbia*.

The *Columbia* was owned and operated by the Herman F. Mehl Excursion Company. The primary stockholder, Capt. Herman F. Mehl, had command of the boat. The boat had been built in 1898 and had three decks of cabins with a pilothouse on top. The *Columbia* was licensed to carry 1,000 passengers at a time, and the steamer began the 1918 season with trips from Peoria and Pekin. There was also a series of 40-mile Saturday trips up the river at a charge of 25¢ and 15¢ for adults and children. Advertisements offered "moonlight dancing excursions," and whole families went to the riverboat for the evening tours.

On July 5, 1918, the South Side Social Club of Pekin scheduled a dance on the steamer *Columbia*. The Peoria, Pekin and Western Railroad was also hosting a family night for its employees. The cost for the cruise was 50¢ for men and 25¢ for women. Captain Mehl and pilot Tom Williams, both veterans of the river, were looking forward to an easy excursion, with those aboard in high spirits and in the mood to be entertained.

The steamboat left Pekin destined for Peoria's Al Fresco Park, a popular amusement park on the banks of the Illinois River boasting a Ferris wheel and concession stands. One hundred people were picked up at Kingston Mines, and the remainder at Pekin. Some 563 tickets had been sold, and between 485 and 530 passengers from Pekin, Peoria, Kingston Mines, Green Valley, Petersburg, and Bloomington crowded the decks and staterooms of the *Columbia* for the festivities, with an additional 20 crew members and a three-man orchestra. The *Colombia* also held a cargo full of fresh coal taken earlier that evening.

The boat left from Pekin on the round-trip excursion on the river at 8:40 p.m. The hour-and-35-minute cruise to Al Fresco Park was uneventful. The guests enjoyed soda, beer, candy, peanuts, and popcorn offered from concession stands and the café, and people danced to the band or walked on the promenade deck. The dance floor on the bottom deck remained open, and many passengers stayed below deck to dance the remainder of the night. The rest crowded the decks and railings, watching through the fog as the silent Illinois River glided by in the darkness. The steamer set off for the return trip to Pekin shortly after 11:00 p.m.

The pilot, Tom Williams, entered a narrow river bend above the village of Wesley City (now Creve Couer). There was a spotty, light fog over the river. Rains the weekend before had caused the water to rise one foot. The river at this site had some treacherous curves, and the eddying river forced the *Columbia* over the western bank. The boat was moving at nearly full speed when it glanced off a submerged stump near the shoreline. The boat pulled sideways, and the trees along the shoreline scraped the white paint along the sides of the ship, breaking several windows on the right side and breaking off railings. Captain Mehl thought they had hit a sandbar and brought the ship to a halt. After the *Columbia* stopped, Tom Williams telegraphed the engine room to reverse the engine. The *Columbia* pulled away from the trees and shoreline and moved slowly out toward the open river. At this point, the boat was only 200 yards from shore. The steamer immediately started listing, and water was flooding the lower level. Captain Mehl descended to the lower deck to look at the possible damage and immediately realized the boat was sinking. He called for the pilot to get them to shore as quickly as possible. Tom Williams headed full steam for the nearby Tazewell County shoreline, but it was too late.

The initial impact was jarring, knocking passengers to the ground and upsetting tables and chairs. Few on board realized the danger, and there were calls from the dance floor for the orchestra to keep playing. For a few moments, the boat was at a standstill. The passengers began to warily examine the damage, and many began to head toward the deck to see the cause of the impact. Suddenly the electrical system in the steamer went out, leaving those aboard in pitch blackness. There was a sudden panic to get to the deck. The exits quickly became crowded with bodies, as parents tried to locate children and other loved ones. The dance floor split across the center, and as water rushed in, the dancers slid across the floor into the crevasse. Passengers began climbing over each other to get to the observation deck above, desperately trying to jump overboard and swim to shore. Captain Mehl shouted orders at the crowd to remain calm and get onto the top deck, but his voice was lost in the melee as the now-panic-stricken mass fought harder to escape the boat. Many were injured in the resulting stampede, with partygoers breaking glass and ripping apart doors in their efforts to escape the interior rooms.

The stump had ripped an 11-foot-long and 2-foot-wide hole through the steel on the bottom of the hull. Captain Mehl chose to back off the submerged tree stump and reverse the boat, a decision that would later be criticized by investigators. As the *Columbia* pulled away, the hole in the bottom of the boat widened and quickly flooded. The result was sudden and dramatic. Water rushed into the hull and quickly began to unbalance the boat. The extra 100 tons of coal in cargo further weighed down the *Columbia*. There was a large crash as the boat collapsed. The steamboat sank within a few moments into 25 feet of water. Eighty-seven people on board drowned within the boat or were pinned under wreckage while trying to escape. At least eight

Here are two scenes of rescuers at the Columbia *wreckage. (Courtesy of Fox Photography.)*

GHOSTS OF THE ILLINOIS RIVER

of the victims were killed by falling debris. Watches recovered from the bodies of two female victims stopped at 12:05 a.m. on July 6, pinpointing the time of the sinking.

The word quickly got out about the sinking of the *Columbia*. Rescuers swarmed onto the scene, trying to herd the still-panicked survivors away from the wreckage. Men, women, and children were pulled from the water and taken to the nearby shoreline. They were facing an uphill battle as the site of the disaster was in pitch darkness. Fog and muffled cries engulfed the rescue volunteers. They worked by groping with their hands in the murky wreckage and taking turns diving into the water. They grabbed in the jumble of arms, legs, and feet, pulling bodies from the wreckage. There was no light that could penetrate the murky water. The dance floor had cracked in the center and dropped down into the hull, trapping the bodies in the deep V created in the middle of the dance floor. Once the dance floor collapsed, there were no upper exits that could be reached. Most of those who survived managed to climb through the upper skylight windows to the top deck.

Most of the 87 bodies were pulled from the sunken hull by these rescuers at frequent intervals throughout the night. The bodies were mainly women and children. The few lanterns available revealed some gruesome sights. The body of a young woman was pulled from the wreckage the hands still holding tightly to a baby buggy. The corpse of a small child was inside. The bodies were placed into baskets, with identifying tags for those who were recognized. They were covered with white sheets and then placed onto barges and taken downstream to Pekin. There was a crush on the riverfront in Pekin, as hysterical family members, roused in the early morning hours, awaited word of loved ones aboard the *Columbia*. They questioned the survivors and waited eagerly for each new report from the rescuers who came at infrequent intervals. Once unloaded in Pekin, the bodies were transported up the cobblestones of Court Street to a temporary morgue set up in the Empire building (vacant building at 337 Court Street). The ambulances could not handle the number of bodies, and delivery trucks and express wagons were put into service. Once in the morgue, the bodies were examined and laid out in rows under white sheets for identification by relatives. All undertakers within a 25-mile radius of Peoria were pressed into service to care for the dead. The home guards patrolled the morgue, and the Red Cross women came to administer to the relatives of the deceased, many of whom were hysterical and fainting at the scene.

When the fog finally cleared the next morning, there was a grim sight on the Illinois River. The forlorn wreckage of the *Columbia* lay listlessly in the water, the collapsed ship a vivid outline against the rising sun. Life preservers, ornamental woodwork, hats, handkerchiefs, and handbags floated around the site. A piece of half-finished knitting and a khaki sweater drifted sadly in the wreck. A pair of elaborate lavender slippers, the needlework partially completed, was also found. The exit sign of the boat, cheerfully calling for those debarking to "Call Again" hung above the companionway. In the checkroom, hats, sweaters, and jackets were pulled from the wreck.

Automobiles from those observing the site lined the banks on both sides of the river. Rowboats and motorboats crowded the water at the scene of the tragedy, with sightseers and volunteers in equal supply. Along the shoreline, hundreds of discarded life preservers lay rooted in the mud.

The funerals from the *Columbia* filled the following week, and recreational activities came to a standstill in Peoria, Pekin, and the surrounding towns and villages. Divers were sent to the wreckage on Saturday morning, as volunteers tore away the top decks. Wreckage with the ship's motto, "Safety First," was brought up from the murky bottoms. Parts of the hull were left in the water as a memorial to those departed and a clear warning to those on the river. The eventual fate of the remnants of the *Columbia*, including the paddle wheel, remains unknown.

Eager for a scapegoat, the people turned against the owner and crew. There were rumors of drunken piloting and substandard construction of the boat. National guardsmen were moved into East Peoria after rumors began regarding lynching for Captain Mehl and Tom Williams. Following an official investigation, the federal court trial concluded that "no evidence of unseaworthiness had been found . . . and the life-saving equipment was found to be in good condition and available." The court concluded that the cause of the sinking and loss of life was due solely to improper seamanship. In the resulting investigation, both Captain Mehl and pilot Tom Williams lost their riverboat licenses. Captain Mehl was assessed a fine of $800 cash and ordered to relinquish the remaining hull of the Columbia.

It was the worst riverboat disaster on the Illinois River. The tragedy of the Columbia brought an end to the excursion steamboat business in the area as the area grieved, stories began to emerge about the sinking.

"I heard someone say that we were so near shore that one could touch the willows with a fishing pole," said survivor William Newman. "Then I felt a smash, like something had hit the bottoms. I saw the music men dive for the windows and called to them to keep playing. They started up and then my girl and I danced twice around the room. Then I felt the boat swing out to the middle of the river and the, it seemed to me that the pilot must have swung her short around and something tore apart. Then it was black . . . I grabbed my girl and got a big gulp of water and than I felt solid floor under me. I pushed up and got air. I broke a window and a fellow reached through and grabbed my girl, then I passed two other women out."

Mrs. Fred Snyder testified during the grand jury investigation that "The first crash sounded just like pushing a crow bar through a rotten board . . . It felt just as if whatever struck the hull of the boat went right through . . . We left and started for the front of the boat. On the way we met Captain Herman Mehl, who said, 'Don't be foolish. We only hit another sandbar in the fog.' We had almost finished three sandwiches when the bells commenced ringing violently, and the woman at the lunch counter, who evidently understood the signals, said 'My God, something has happened.' We started again for the front of the boat, and on the way saw men looking down the forward hatchway. 'Nosey-like I stopped to look down and I saw water rushing in with a sound like Niagara Falls." She ran up to the dance floor, and as she got there the boat listed toward the Peoria shore, and the people dancing began to slide into the water. They were fighting with each other to get out, and people were calling frantically with cries to save their babies or children. The lights went out, and Mrs. Snyder testified she was thrown into water up to her hips. She swam and floated to the White House crossing one mile below the site of the wreck, where she was rescued.

Thomas E. Miller reported that he was in the first deck bar when the boat dipped the first time. He saw water on the barroom floor and began running toward the stairs, yelling at those around him to get to the top of the Columbia. He went to the third deck and grabbed a splashboard near the paddle wheel. He was later rescued from the site. He estimated the boat was 30–40 feet from the Peoria shoreline at the time of the crash.

Rudolph Lohmann reported that after the initial impact, he retuned to the bar and there was water on the floor. He ran up the stairs toward the top deck. Once on the third deck, he grabbed an iron post on the stairway. The floor disappeared beneath him, and the middle of the boat caved in on itself. The boat rocked over sideways, and there was a loud crash with cries and screams rising from beneath him.

Guy McIntire, a steamfitter, related the following:

I was sitting near the orchestra talking to the trap drummer when the boat gave a lurch. Then it started to list and some one said it was going down. I grabbed my wife and we fought our way to the high side of the dance deck, which now leaned at an angle of 45 degrees. The water was rising, and people clung to me, almost pulling me into the water. I managed to help some to a hand hold, but a large beam cut me off from safety. I assisted some in climbing over, others in getting under and to places of safety. Men struggled about me, one kicked me in the face and cut my lip, and I received a blow on the head, but we clung to the boat and some one struck a match and gave me a view of the surrounding that helped me and my wife reach safety until a skiff arrived. The water was up to our socks and still rising when we got out.

Entire families were lost together in the wreckage. The family of Clyde Witcher of 109 Fayette Street had gone on the steamship together. Clyde, his wife, and their two children died holding onto each other for support, and their bodies were later recovered.

On July 11, 1918, the hull of the steamship *Columbia* came to the surface while attempts were being made to remove it. The dislodged hulk floated downstream about a hundred yards and grounded itself in a sandbar. It remained there for a few weeks until a group of volunteers split apart the boat and removed the wreckage.

With the many tragic and gruesome deaths associated with the sinking of the *Columbia*, it is hardly surprising that reports of ghosts have surfaced surrounding the ill-fated ship. One of the many stories that have been reported is that of a phantom steamboat seen in the vicinity of the crash. The ship appears briefly in the heavy fog along the river and just as quickly dissipates. Those sighting the vessel have reported hearing the faint sounds of the calliope just before the boat vanishes. Another popular report is of a ghostly green light that is said to appear in the depths of the river at the place where the boat sunk. The story is that the light is from those still searching for an exit or trying to find a loved one on the ship. Legend reports that when occupants on a boat see the green light they need to quickly leave the river, as that is the light of those departed trying to pull them to their deaths.

The Swain Dynasty and the *Julia Belle Swain*

David M. Swain and the Swain family owned and operated boats on the Illinois River beginning around 1880. Ships at that time were commonly named after family members, and the Swain family were no exception, with the *David*, *Fred*, and *Percy Swain* all appearing. However, there was a local superstition that if the name of the boat contained the initial M, the vessel was doomed to sink, taking all hands down with it. This taboo of the M was well respected in boating lore of the time, and the Swain family never used that initial on any of its ships.

In 1890, David Swain brought his first steamboat, the *Borealis Rex*, to the Illinois River. The boat operated between Peoria and LaSalle. In 1904, David brought the *Verne Swain* to Peoria to run excursion to the St. Louis world's fair, and in 1906, the *David Swain* appeared. This excursion boat was used as Pres. Theodore Roosevelt's flagship during his trip down the Mississippi River. On August 9, 1909, the *Fred Swain* caught fire and was destroyed.

The final and largest boat owned by the Swain family was the *Julia Belle Swain*, which was built in 1913 and named for the daughter of Capt. Percy Swain. The boat was built for service on the Gulf of Mexico and was brought to Peoria in 1916. The boat was sold in 1924 and later destroyed by fire. The Swain era on the Illinois River was over by World War I.

In 1971, a new *Julia Belle Swain* was christened and docked at the Peoria waterfront. The boat was owned, designed, and built by Capt. Dennis Trone. The engines, hull, superstructure, pilot wheel, and pilothouse were all salvaged from a ferry boat called the *City of Baton Rouge*. The pleasure paddle wheeler was built to take daily excursions onto the Illinois River and to provide two-day trips from Peoria to Starved Rock Lodge and State Park. The *Julia Belle* was operated by the Sangamon Packet Company and piloted by Capt. Roy Boyd. The boat could accommodate 400 passengers and cruise 12–14 miles per hour.

The new *Julia Belle* was rumored to be the home of restless spirits that had been transported from the *City of Baton Rouge*. During one reported encounter aboard the *Julia Belle Swain* in the 1980s, a young woman and her family went for a moonlit cruise down the river. The woman left her family in the downstairs dining area and sought some fresh air on the top deck. As she climbed the stairs and walked around the upper deck, she was surprised to notice an older woman standing at the back, watching the river glide by in the darkness. The lady was wearing an old-fashioned dress of the type popular in the early 19th century and had her hair up in a bun. The young woman thought she was a historical reenactor on board for the evening entertainment and walked toward her with the intention of complimenting the accuracy and beauty of her gown. As she came closer to the woman, she noticed that the lady seemed to be standing off the ground, as her feet and lower half were hardly visible. The young woman took a few more steps and the figure turned to look at her. As it did so, it seemed to disappear into the night air, leaving a faint odor of perfume. The young woman was frightened and quickly ran back downstairs to tell her family what she had seen, and they alerted some of the workers aboard. A search of the boat was hastily conducted for the woman, but no one of that description had been seen or could be found. The young woman realized she had just had her first encounter with one of the ghosts of the Illinois River.

The Legend of Nee Nee Wah

There are many Native American tales associated with the Illinois River, and one of these is set in Peoria. According to legend, Nee Nee Wah was a beautiful young Native American maiden of the Peoria tribe. She met and fell in love with a handsome young buck in the enemy Potawatomi tribe. Neither of the families approved of the match, and Nee Nee Wah was kept under close guard to ensure she did not run off with the young buck. Eventually the lovers became desperate and vowed to escape their families and run away together to start a new life. Nee Nee Wah was reluctant to leave behind her family, but eventually the young man persuaded her to meet him so they could elope together across Peoria Lake. He waited until a night he knew there would be a full moon to light their way and persuaded Nee Nee Wah to meet him on the bluff at his signal. Nee Nee Wah heard her lover's signal and slipped from her village into the darkness. The couple met on the water's edge and got into a birch bark canoe to cross Peoria Lake. Unfortunately for the pair, the young maiden had been seen leaving the camp. Her parents were alerted to her absence and assembled a search party to pursue the lovers across the lake. The young buck canoed as fast as he could, but they both knew they could not escape their pursuers. Rather than risk capture and separation, the two young lovers made a pact to remain together always. Holding onto each other, they jumped into the murky darkness of the Illinois River. The waters swallowed them up, and both lovers drowned in Peoria Lake. It is said that if young lovers are boating in Peoria Lake during a full moon, they can hear the sound of canoe oars swiftly hitting the water, followed by the splash of the two young lovers jumping to their death.

A New Chapter

A good ghost story gives the reader the chance to go back in time, a time when fairy tales were still possible and the cozy warmth of home was a retreat from the cold darkness. The ghost story conjures up half-forgotten images of spooks and goblins from childhood, a jumble of golden memories of things that go bump in the night. From riding with Ichabod Crane down a lonely hallow trying to escape the headless horseman, to visiting the ghosts of Ebenezer Scrooge, all the way to the ravaged and fanciful phantasms of Edgar Allen Poe, the formative years are shaped by stories of ghouls, spirits and specters, monsters and legends. Like many cities, Peoria is home to many beloved ghost stories and tales that continue to fascinate both the young and old in the community.

At one point in its history, Peoria was known as the "City of the Dead," as the bones of the earliest ancestors routinely surfaced in the expansion of the downtown area. Peoria's turbulent history and diverse culture make the city a popular site for supernatural activity. Peoria continues to delight with tales of haunted cemeteries, old insane asylums, ghostly hospitals, and legends of the restless, wandering specters of some of the city's most prominent citizens. Whether one comes for business or for pleasure, the ghosts of haunted Peoria are waiting.

Discover Thousands of Local History Books
Featuring Millions of Vintage Images

Arcadia Publishing, the leading local history publisher in the United States, is committed to making history accessible and meaningful through publishing books that celebrate and preserve the heritage of America's people and places.

Find more books like this at
www.arcadiapublishing.com

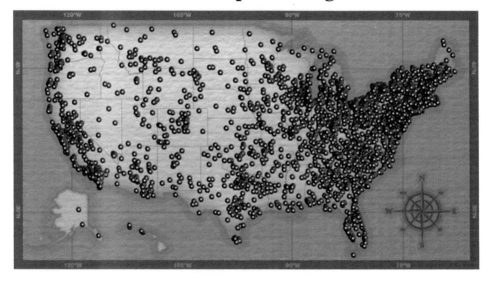

Search for your hometown history, your old stomping grounds, and even your favorite sports team.